Bookseller as Rogue

American University Studies

Series IV
English Language and Literature

Vol. 28

PETER LANG
New York · Berne · Frankfurt am Main

Bookseller as Rogue:

John Almon and the Politics of Eighteenth-Century Publishing

Deborah D. Rogers

«... the person ... is Almon, whom I know and
have found to be a rogue.» – Horace Walpole

PETER LANG
New York · Berne · Frankfurt am Main

Library of Congress Cataloging in Publication Data

Rogers, Deborah D.:
Bookseller as Rogue.

(American University Studies. Series IV, English
Language and Literature; vol. 28)
Bibliography: p.
Includes index.
1. Almon, John, 1737–1805. 2. Booksellers and
bookselling – Great Britain – Biography. 3. Booksellers
and bookselling – England – London – History – 18th century.
4. Publishers and publishing – England – London – History –
18th century. 5. Pamphlets – Publishing – England – London –
History – 18th century. 6. Great Britain – Politics and
government – 1760–1820. I. Title. II. Series.
Z325.A53R63 1986 070.5'092'4 [B] 86-2831
ISBN 0-8204-0221-4

CIP-Kurztitelaufnahme der Deutschen Bibliothek

Rogers, Deborah D.:
Bookseller as Rogue: John Almon and the Politics
of Eighteenth-Century Publishing / Deborah D. Rogers. –
New York; Berne; Frankfurt am Main: Lang,
1986.
(American University Studies: Ser. 4, English
Language and Literature; Vol. 28)
ISBN 0-8204-0221-4

NE: American University Studies / 04

© Peter Lang Publishing, Inc., New York 1986

Printed by Lang Druck, Inc., Liebefeld/Berne (Switzerland)

TO MARVIN AND MARILYN ROGERS
AND TO THE MEMORY OF RAE ROGERS

Contents

Preface

The effect of politics on eighteenth-century authors and literature seems fairly obvious. It is often pointed out, for example, that the political orientation of *The Beggar's Opera* was responsible for the subsequent banning of *Polly* from the stage and that after the Playhouse Act of 1737, Fielding turned to journalism and to novels. Many important eighteenth-century authors, such as Defoe, Swift, Addison, and Steele, were actively engaged in political pamphleteering. In addition, it was not unusual for men of letters to be statesmen: Defoe helped negotiate the Act of Union between England and Scotland; Prior was instrumental in negotiating both the Peace of Ryswick and the Peace of Utrecht, and Addison was Secretary of State.

Examples of the impact of politics on eighteenth-century authors could, of course, be multiplied. Less widely recognized, however, is the effect of politics on the booksellers of the period. When I first planned this study, I intended to analyze how political pressures on booksellers affected the nature of eighteenth-century English literature. It soon became apparent, however, that such a project would be overwhelming: It would have to be situated against the background of the shift in the financing of literature from patronage to pay, yet this transition has received practically no attention.

In general, surprisingly little has been written about patronage of the arts in eighteenth-century England. Most considerations of eighteenth-century patronage have appeared within the context of separate examinations of individual authors who were either recipients or supplicants. The only full-length treatment of the subject, Michael Foss's study of the patronage of literature, painting, music, and architecture from the Restoration to 1750, has been aptly characterized by Paul Korshin as falling "somewhere between B. Sprague Allen's *Tides in English Taste* and . . . recent studies of representative artists. . . ."[1]

Although the main concern of Bertrand Goldgar's excellent study *Walpole and the Wits* is the relationship between politics and literature during the Walpole administration, Goldgar does consider Walpole's failure to provide patronage to men of letters as a major motif of opposition propaganda.[2] Similarly, Kenneth Greene persuasively argues that while authors continued to seek government patronage during the Walpole ministry, Walpole was generally indifferent to their efforts. If Walpole dispensed a considerable sum of money to hacks who wrote propaganda, he rewarded literary figures with only enough to encourage their vain pursuit of ministerial support.[3]

Studies of patronage that cover the entire eighteenth century include essays by Robert Halsband and by Paul Korshin.[4] Both Halsband and Korshin describe different types of literary patronage, such as governmental support and subscription publication. Korshin takes dedications into account, while Halsband adds "public patronage" (p. 187).

Most examinations of eighteenth-century patronage, then, confine themselves to the first half of the century; those that do span the period are largely concerned to classify different categories of support. All these studies almost overlook the transition from patronage to pay. Even the common assumption that during the period, booksellers became more important as patronage became less obtainable has never been fully documented.[5] Astonishingly, scholars of the period have virtually ignored the commercialization of literature.

Given this situation, it seemed useful to concentrate on a single bookseller in an attempt to contribute to our understanding of eighteenth-century publishing history. In fact, I became increasingly convinced that only with many such studies will we be able to reach significant conclusions about the complex transformation of the economic basis of literature that occurred during the century.

I have chosen to focus on John Almon because his situation provides a particularly appropriate point of reference in terms of my original concern with the relationship between politics, bookselling, and literature: According to his contemporaries, Almon was "connected by his writings and his abilities with the politics of this country [England] and . . . has united the profession of a man of letters with that of a bookseller."[6]

Almon was accorded considerable importance by eighteenth and nineteenth-century sources, but today is remembered dimly at best. In fact, until now, there has been no full-length examination of this prominent eighteenth-century figure whom the *Gentleman's Magazine* regarded as the most important political publisher of his day:

> Pamphlet after pamphlet was transmitted to the press through the medium of Mr. Almon, who . . . was countenanced by the protection of the most respectable leaders of the party in Opposition to the Ministry. . . . Mr. Almon soon ranked foremost in the list of political publishers.[7]

The decline of Almon's reputation becomes striking if we trace the Almon entries in different editions of the same reference work. An encyclopaedia is ideally suited for this purpose because through the years, it is revised specifically to bring it "up to date," to reflect the attitudes of the times. For example, the 1875 edition of the *Encyclopaedia Britannica*, in a rather long account, portrayed Almon as a "political pamphleteer and publisher of considerable note," who had a "very important influence on the political history of this country [England]." Yet by 1910 the *Encyclopaedia* described him simply as an "English political pamphleteer and publisher." The 1936 version is half as long as previous entries. By 1973, a short item in the *Encyclopaedia* characterized Almon as a "parliamentary reporter and political writer"—that is, as a hack.

An analysis of standard reference sources and their relationships to one another can help determine how and why Almon's reputation diminished. It seems somewhat ironic that, to the degree that he emphasized topical concerns in his *Memoirs*, Almon himself may be responsible for his current status. This is because any attempt to recover information about Almon must in some measure depend on his self-perception as it is presented in his *Memoirs* and perpetuated in further accounts. For instance, most discussions of printers for this period begin with Plomer. Plomer's description of Almon is ostensibly derived from Almon's *Memoirs*, Timperley, and the DNB.[8] A brief chronological survey of Plomer's sources would start with the *Memoirs*, where Almon pays scant attention to his early activities, family matters, personal affairs, poetical works, or literary collections. Instead, Almon supplies a fairly detailed record of his political connections and legal difficulties. Subsequent reference works retain Almon's emphasis. The information in Timperley, Plomer's second source, is almost entirely derived from the *Memoirs* and largely appropriates its language. The third source under consideration, the DNB, seems to be based mostly on Timperley. However, the DNB also relies on the portrayal of Almon in *Public Characters*. It is perhaps worth mentioning that a hostile article on Almon in Chalmers describes this biography as "a very flattering life, evidently contributed by himself."[9] Although I can find no evidence for this accusation, if true, it would further corroborate the theory that Almon's self-conception may have contributed to his present obscurity.

More recent sources likewise depend directly or through some intermediate work (usually Plomer, Timperley, or the DNB) on Almon's autobiography. Thus, it is hardly surprising that most estimates of Almon consist of little more than his own version of his activities. The present study will therefore attempt to reconstruct, as far as possible, Almon's life and career. First, however, something needs to be said about the sources for this investigation.

The computer-based Eighteenth-Century Short Title Catalogue (hereafter, ESTC) greatly facilitated the registering of works issued under Almon's imprint. (See appendix.) In addition, there are three major collections of Almon's papers.[10] The Almon manuscripts in the British Library consist of Almon's various correspondence from 1766 to his death in 1805.[11] Scholars have examined these manuscripts largely with regard to Wilkes.

Archival research for this project will also make extensive use of two collections of Almon's papers that have been relatively ignored. Both collections are of immense value, not only for the light they throw on Almon—they contain a wealth of information about many important eighteenth-century politicians who figured in his network of relationships.

The Almon collection in the William R. Perkins Library of Duke University contains the correspondence between Almon and John Calcraft. These papers, which date from 1769 until Calcraft's death in 1772, are primarily concerned with politics.[12]

Even more surprising than the neglect of the Almon holdings at Duke is the neglect of the Almon collection in the New-York Historical Society (hereafter, NYHS), which consists of one hundred and fifty miscellaneous items dating from 1770 to 1805. According to Mr. Thomas Dunnings, Curator of Manuscripts, no reader has examined these documents since the Society acquired them in 1936. Although the manuscripts are in poor condition—pages are actually crumbling—they are bound in a manner that prevents duplication. Therefore these papers (mere fragments, drafts, and memoranda though they may be) take on added significance.

In what follows, for the period after 1766, I depend to a large extent on unpublished manuscript sources, especially those which are deteriorating. In the interest of preservation, these will be quoted from at length. Except in titles, where capitalization has been modernized, original spelling (even when idiosyncratic), capitalization, and punctuation have been retained.

Notes

[1] *The Age of Patronage* (Ithaca: Cornell University Press, 1972); Paul Korshin, rev. of *The Age of Patronage* by Michael Foss, *Eighteenth-Century Studies*, 7 (1973), p. 102.

[2] *Walpole and the Wits* (Lincoln: University of Nebraska Press, 1976). See also Mabel Hessler, "The Literary Opposition to Sir Robert Walpole," Diss. University of Chicago 1934.

[3] "Sir Robert Walpole and Literary Patronage," Diss. Columbia University 1964. Discussions that include a consideration of eighteenth-century patronage with reference to the professionalization of authorship are: A.S. Collins, *Authorship in the Days of Johnson* (1927; rpt. Clifton, New Jersey: A.M. Kelley, 1973); Diana Laurenson, "Origins of Authorship and Patronage" in Diana Laurenson and Alan Swingewood, *The Sociology of Literature* (London: MacGibbon and Kee, 1972), pp. 93–116, and Laurenson, "The Professionalization of the Writer" in Laurenson and Swingewood, pp. 117–39. It should be mentioned that, at least as far as the eighteenth century is concerned, Laurenson's accounts are highly unreliable. For example, Laurenson is under the impression that the Restoration occurred in 1688, the year of the Glorious Revolution, and that Addison became Secretary of State in 1721, two years after his death.

[4] Robert Halsband, "Literary Patronage in Eighteenth-Century England" [abstract only], in *Expression, Communication and Experience in Literature and Language*, ed. Ronald Popperwell, Proc. of the XII Congress of the International Federation for Modern Languages and Literatures, 20–26 Aug. 1972 (Leeds: Modern Humanities Research Association, 1973), pp. 186–87; Paul Korshin, "Types of Eighteenth-Century Literary Patronage," *Eighteenth-Century Studies*, 7 (1974), 453–73.

[5] See, for example, Ian Watt, *The Rise of the Novel* (1957; rpt. Berkeley: University of California Press, 1967), pp. 52–59; Laurenson, "Origins of Authorship and Patronage," pp. 111 and 115; Laurenson, "Professionalization of the Writer," pp. 117–18; Halsband, p. 187; Foss, pp. 66 and 83; Alexandre Beljame, *Men of Letters and the English Public in the Eighteenth Century*, trans. E.O. Lorimer, ed. and introd. Bonamy Dobrée (France, 1881; rpt. London: Kegan Paul, 1948).

[6] "Mr. Almon," *Public Characters of 1803–1804*, 6 (1804), 121.

[7] "Obituary, with Anecdotes of Remarkable Persons," *Gentleman's Magazine*, 75 (1805), 1179.

[8] H.R. Plomer, G.H. Bushnell, and E.R. Dix, *A Dictionary of Printers and Booksellers who were at Work in England Scotland and Ireland from 1726 to 1775* (London: Printed for the Bibliographical Society at Oxford University Press, 1932); John Almon, *Memoirs of a Late Eminent Bookseller* (London, 1790; facsim. New York: Garland, 1974); C.H. Timperley, *Encyclopedia of Literary and Typographical Anecdote* (1839; 1842 edn. in facsim. New York: Garland, 1977); Edward Smith, "Almon, John," *Dictionary of National Biography* (1885).

[9] Alexander Chalmers, "Almon (John)," *The General Biographical Dictionary* (1812), II, 36n.

[10] Other manuscript sources are located in the Public Record Office (Treasury Board, Treasury Solicitor Papers No. 765 and Audit Office and Pipe Office Papers, Accounts, Various, Nos. 1398–99).

[11] Add. MS. 20733. The British Library also has two assignments of copyright to Almon (Add. MS. 38728 fo. 194 and Add. MS. 38730 fo. 10) as well as several letters

from Almon to the Duke of Newcastle (Add. MS. 32939 fo. 242 and Add. MS. 32959 fo. 233). In addition, among the Wilkes papers in the British Library are many letters from Almon. Written during the time Wilkes was in France, these are of the utmost importance because they serve to round out the known correspondence between Almon and Wilkes (Add. MS. 30868 fos. 136–37; Add. MS. 30869 fos. 95, 106–107, 110, 119, 123, 128, 139, 144, 151, 153, 157; Add. MS. 30870 fo. 107; Add. MS. 30875 fo. 4). For the most part, these are Almon's unpublished responses to the letters that appear in his *Correspondence of the Late John Wilkes, with his Friends, Printed from the Original Manuscripts, in which are Introduced Memoirs of his Life* (London: Printed for Richard Phillips by Nichols and Son, 1805), III, 123–150 (hereafter cited as Almon's biography and letters of Wilkes).

[12] Perkins MS XVIII-E.

Acknowledgements

For kindly granting permission to quote from their manuscript collections, I wish to thank the William R. Perkins Library of Duke University, the British Library Board, and the New-York Historical Society.

I would gratefully like to acknowledge the assistance of Herb Sloan, who scrupulously read this work in draft, and of Eileen McIlvaine and her fellow librarians at Columbia University. I am also indebted to my teachers at Columbia, especially to Otis Fellows, who encouraged and inspired me, to Terry Belanger, who suggested the topic, and to John H. Middendorf, who has always helped me, not only with this project, but every step of the way. I owe additional thanks to the University of Maine for the award of a summer faculty research grant to complete this undertaking and to Steven Youra and the rest of my colleagues for their continuing advice and friendship.

This book could never have been written without the support and understanding of William H. Bristow, Jr. I am also pleased to express my appreciation to Erica Heller, to Warren Johnson, to Barbara Millman, to Mollie Leff, and to Michael, Judy, and Glenn Rogers. My deepest gratitude is recorded in the dedication.

Chronology

(Almon's works are listed separately in the bibliography. Works published under Almon's imprint are catalogued in the appendix.)

1737	December 17, John Almon born in Liverpool.
1743	Almon's father dies.
1744	Almon's mother dies; moves to North Meales in Lancashire.
1751	Disappearance of Almon's brother Francis; in March becomes apprenticed to Robert Williamson.
1758	September, goes abroad.
1759	Moves to London.
1760	October 27, marries Elizabeth Jackson; is employed as journeyman printer.
1761	January, becomes Say's assistant on the *Gazetteer*.
1762	Meets Earl Temple and John Wilkes.
1763	Establishes own bookshop at 178 Piccadilly.
1764	Appointed official bookseller to the Coterie.
1765	May 1, prosecuted for publishing *A Letter Concerning Libels*; July, charges dropped.
1770	June 2, prosecuted for libel (*London Museum* trial); November 28, sentenced to put up £800 security.
1771	Participates in Printer's Case.
1781	June, retires to Box Moor, Hertfordshire; August 31, wife dies.
1784	September, returns to London; second marriage.
1786	Prosecuted for libels on William Pitt the younger published in the *General Advertiser*; fined £150.

1788	Prosecuted for libelling the King in the *General Advertiser*; fails to appear for sentencing and is outlawed.
1789	Flees to France/ Box Moor
1792	March, imprisoned in the King's Bench.
1793	April, outlawry charges reversed.
1805	December 12, dies at Box Moor.

1
Early Years, Relationships, and Business

Since little is known about Almon, it seems appropriate to begin by discussing his early years. This preliminary chapter will therefore examine Almon's childhood, his youth, and the beginning of his career. In this connection, it will be necessary to analyze in some detail Almon's relationship with the man who was perhaps his most influential contact during this formative period—Richard Grenville, Earl Temple. Finally, the importance of this friendship will become apparent: Temple brought Almon into contact with the political leaders who would establish him as bookseller to the Opposition.

Although several allusions to Almon's personal affairs are scattered throughout his works, generally speaking, we have few records of Almon's childhood. Even his autobiography, which does provide a genealogy, is largely concerned with his career.[1] Yet, with the aid of contemporary texts and relevant manuscripts, the general outlines of his life can be tentatively established.

In 1728 John Almon, the father of the subject of this study, left his Irish birthplace to seek his fortune in Liverpool. His beginnings were auspicious. By 1731 he had married the former Isabella Thompson and, through his wife, shortly thereafter took possession of estates in Lancashire and of at least five houses in Liverpool. It was in one of these houses—the house on Moore Street—that his namesake, John Almon, was born on 17 December 1737.[2]

1

The early loss of his family is of major importance in any biographical consideration of Almon. While he was still a child, three of Almon's siblings died in infancy. But the death of both his parents was no doubt more devastating. A broad but unavoidably incomplete survey of documents and obituary columns has failed to reveal any of the particulars of these sad occasions. There is, however, no reason to doubt the sole account of the death of Almon's parents, which appears in his *Memoirs*. Here Almon summarily dismisses the death of his father with the information that the elder Almon began a maritime career in 1743 and was soon presumed to be dead. Almon takes more notice of the death of his mother, which occurred the following year: Returning from a trip to Ireland, where she had been visiting her in-laws, Isabella Almon set out on an ill-fated voyage back to Liverpool aboard the Fame. When the ship was reported missing, Almon entertained "flattering hopes . . . that this vessel might possibly be driven to the northward or southward, and perhaps have put into some distant port."[3] But these hopes were disappointed, as pieces of the wreck washed ashore, gradually revealing the story of this calamity.

Thus, by the time Almon was seven, he and his twelve-year-old brother, Francis, had become orphans. The future probably appeared frightening and uncertain to the two children, who went to live with their maternal grandmother, Margaret Thompson, in North Meales in Lancashire.[4] Although we know little about Almon's early training, it is generally supposed that he received his education in Lancashire at Warrington.[5]

After weighing much fragmentary evidence, I have come to the conclusion that John Sykes was Almon's teacher. For one thing, in his letter to Almon of 11 March 1778, Sykes discussed a former student.[6] In fact, when Almon reminisced about Sykes, he described him as his "preceptor."[7] In this respect, Almon's poem "To Mr. Sykes" is of biographical interest. Here Almon addressed Sykes as "the pupil's fav'rite and the Muse's friend."[8] Almon's lifelong correspondence with Sykes, some of which is preserved in the British Library, may be taken for evidence of their continued friendship.[9]

In 1751, when Almon was fourteen, he experienced still another loss. His only surviving sibling, Francis, disappeared on a voyage to the West Indies. Like his father, Francis was soon thought to be dead.[10] For Almon these days must have been bleak and disheartening. A change of scene was in order, and some time in March, an unidentified uncle arranged for Almon to be apprenticed to the Liverpool bookseller, binder, and printer, Robert Williamson.[11]. This would provide him with valuable training for the years ahead.

Nevertheless, in September, 1758, in much the same manner as his father and older brother, Almon left Liverpool to try the seafaring life. According to the *Gentleman's Magazine*:

> the trammels of business not suiting his soaring talents, he quitted his original employ . . . and tried his fortune on the Ocean. But here he was disappointed. The labours of an ordinary Seaman were by far more severe than he expected; and he took the earliest opportunity of visiting the Metropolis. . . .[12]

In 1759, after having seen something of the Continent, Almon moved to London. Among the Almon papers in the New-York Historical Society is a poem in which Almon favorably compares his new home to the famous cities of antiquity:

> Not Rome herself so fam'd in song
> By classic bards sung o'er & o'er
> Not Athens in her Attic tongue
> Nor Memphis in her ancient lore
> Shall with our London now compare.[13]

Shortly after his move to the city, Almon took a wife. On 27 October 1760, John Almon and Elizabeth Jackson were married by Almon's friend Charles Churchill.[14]

As we might expect, Churchill's works were among the first to be associated with Almon. From 1763, the year Almon would establish his own business, until Churchill's premature death in November, 1764, all of Churchill's works were issued with Almon's name (among others) on the imprint.[15] It may have been through Churchill that Almon met the poet Robert Lloyd. Lloyd and Churchill, who were close friends, were both associated with the Nonsense Club (of which William Cowper was a member) around this time.[16] Apparently Almon was also acquainted with Goldsmith.[17]

During these early years, Almon found work as a journeyman printer with John Watts, in Wild Court, Lincoln's Inn Fields.[18] It was here, in one of the most important printing houses in the city, that Almon was initiated into the exciting world of the London trade. At the same time, Almon was pleased to observe a connection—however remote—to Benjamin Franklin. Almon remarked that he

> happened in the house of one of the masters he worked for, to be put into the same frame (a technical term signifying situation) in which Dr. *Benjamin Franklin* had worked some years before.[19]

Almon provides few further details about his experience at Watts's. But since Almon arrived on the scene shortly after Franklin's departure, the atmosphere must have been similar to that described in Franklin's fuller account. Franklin objected to his fellow employees, who were "great Guzzlers of Beer":

> At my first Admission into this Printing House, I took to working at Press. . . . I drank only Water; the other Workmen, near 50 in Number, were great Guzzlers of Beer. . . . We had an Alehouse Boy who attended always in the House to supply the Workmen. My Companion at the Press, drank every day a Pint before Breakfast, a Pint at Breakfast with his Bread and Cheese; a Pint between Breakfast and Dinner; a Pint at Dinner; a Pint in the Afternoon about Six o'Clock, and another when he had done his Day's-Work. . . . He . . . had 4 or 5 Shillings to pay out of his Wages every Saturday Night for that muddling Liquor. . . .
>
> Watts after some Weeks desiring to have me in the Composing Room, I left the Pressmen. A new *Bienvenu* or Sum for Drink, being 5 s., was demanded of me by the Compositors. I thought it an Imposition. . . . The Master thought so too, and forbad my Paying it. I stood

out two or three Weeks, was accordingly considered as an Excommunicate, and had so many little Pieces of private Mischief done me, by mixing my Sorts, transposing my Pages, breaking my Matter, &c. &c. if I were ever so little out of the Room . . . that notwithstanding the Master's Protection, I found myself oblig'd to comply and pay the Money; convinc'd of the Folly of being on ill Terms with those one is to live with continually.[20]

After regaining his standing with the workmen, Franklin, in typical fashion, attempted to reform them:

I propos'd some reasonable Alterations in their Chapel Laws, and carried them against all Opposition.[21] From my Example a great Part of them, left their muddling Breakfast of Beer and Bread and Cheese, finding they could with me be supply'd from a neighbouring House with a large Porringer of hot Water-gruel. . . .[22]

Although we may never know whether Almon was a beer guzzler or a porridge eater, as previously mentioned, he must have been working in an environment similar to Franklin's. Considering Almon's prolific output, however, it is probable that, like Franklin, Almon abstained. In fact, for Almon, Franklin may have served as a model of just what the printer could become. After all, the London trade (perhaps through Franklin's old friend Strahan), must have already been circulating stories about Franklin, who, by the 1760's, was already a famous, successful Pennsylvania agent in Great Britain.[23]

Like Franklin, Almon soon discovered a talent for writing. During these years, Almon was frequently employed as a political pamphleteer. His first acknowledged work, *The Conduct of a Late Noble Commander Examined*, dealt with the alleged cowardice of Lord George Sackville (later Germain) during the August, 1759 Battle of Minden, where Sackville repeatedly delayed executing orders for the British calvary to advance against the French. Almon's investigation, which was published in September of 1759, supposedly influenced the popular attitude toward Sackville and his court-martial, which took place the following year.[24]

5

The success of Almon's early productions soon attracted the notice of Charles Green Say, printer and proprietor of the *Gazetteer*. In need of a writer to compete with Goldsmith, who was contributing to the *Public Ledger*, Say hired Almon in January, 1761.[25] Contemporaries observed this rivalry:

> Mr. Newberry engaged Dr. Goldsmith to furnish articles, and in it originated his "Chinese Letters;" the first letter was printed on the 24th day of January 1760.
>   The design on this new paper was acknowledged by its proprietors to rival the Gazetteer. This avowal alarmed Mr. Say, the printer, very much; he therefore, without any loss of time, engaged Mr. Almon, at a handsome salary, to assist him.[26]

Almon's articles perfectly suited the liberal viewpoint of the *Gazetteer*. Indeed, Robert Haig credits Almon with both increasing the popularity and enhancing the quality of this publication during his tenure as Say's assistant.[27] Under signatures like "Independent Whig" and "Lucius," Almon regularly wrote political letters for Say's paper.[28] These included pieces that dealt with the resignations of Legge, Devonshire, Newcastle, Temple, and Pitt.

Precisely at the point when Almon began writing, the country was about to undergo one of its most politically chaotic and unsettling periods. From the accession of George III onward, the 1760s were marked by numerous ministerial changes. Much has been made of events leading to Pitt's resignation. Pitt, who had conducted the Seven Years' War brilliantly, wanted to continue the hostilities. But Bute, the King's favorite, who had become Secretary of State in 1761, insisted upon negotiating an end to the War. To their dismay, Pitt and his brother-in-law, Temple, who had demanded that the War be extended to include Spain, learned that peace was at hand. They both resigned on 5 October 1761.[29] Such was the charged atmosphere in which Almon was writing.

Reflecting on his efforts at this time, Almon somewhat hyperbolically recalled Pitt's dependence on his "volunteer pen":

Whoever recollects the period, must have observed the prodigious streams of abuse which were poured upon Mr. *Pitt*, in all the channels of conveyance to the public; while his friends, for a long time, seemed to be unaccountably indolent and indifferent. The fact is, Mr. *Almon's* volunteer pen, was the only one exercised on that side for several months.[30]

However exaggerated these claims may be, Almon nonetheless championed Pitt's cause on repeated occasions.

Of Almon's publications on behalf of Pitt, his *Review of Mr. Pitt's Administration* is of greatest interest here: Almon's career as a political bookseller may be properly said to have begun when this widely noticed chronicle of Pitt's activities aroused the interest of the man to whom it was dedicated, Richard Grenville, Earl Temple.[31] Apparently Temple was so pleased with Almon's work that he sent for him. As a young man, Almon must have been flattered by the nobleman's attention. In his *Memoirs* he characterized his first interview with Temple as the "moment [from which he] was honoured with his Lordship's favor and countenance, publicly and privately" (p. 15). Eager to capitalize on his opportunities, Almon aligned his interests squarely with Lord Temple's.

Until he met Temple, Almon was just another hack journalist. After making Temple's acquaintance, however, he started to emerge as a significant political writer and publisher. Almon's association with Temple ended only with Temple's death in 1779.[32] During this interval, Almon was dubbed "Temple's man."[33] As such, the bookseller was a frequent figure at Pall Mall and Stowe. (To my knowledge, Almon's earliest reference to these visits to Temple appears in his letter to Wilkes of 23 October 1764.)[34] Almon retrospectively described his closeness to Temple in the draft of a letter dated 6 September 1804. Here Almon reflected, "I think I may say without vanity that no man now alive was more in Temple's confidence from the year 1762 till his death & in M^r W's [Wilkes's] also."[35]

Almon drew heavily on his friendship with Temple. It was through Temple that Almon met such powerful members of the Opposition as Newcastle, Rockingham, and Pitt. Besides introducing Almon to these established Whig leaders, Temple also introduced him to John Wilkes just at the time when Wilkes was becoming increasingly radical. In his *Memoirs* Almon describes how he was presented to these important politicians:

> Lord *Temple* carried him to the Duke of *Newcastle*, to make known to his Grace the author of some letters which Mr. *Almon* had written in the Gazetteer, at the time of the Duke's resignation.[36] His Grace expressed himself in terms of the warmest friendship, gave him many thanks, acknowledged the great pleasure he had received every day in reading those letters; that they contained his own sentiments exactly, and much more to the same effect. Lord *Temple* afterwards made him known to the Duke of *Devonshire*, the Marquis of *Rockingham*, &c. Mr. *Pitt* he saw at Lord *Temple's* in Pall-mall, where he did not fail to pay his devoirs once a week at least, and was always admitted. Through the same interest he became known to Mr. *Wilkes*, and many other gentlemen who were at that time in opposition to the court (p. 15).

Almon's political alliances soon became well known, as the following lines from a contemporary poem *The Booksellers* would seem to indicate: "*Almon* of late has got himself a name,/ But 'tis to W------s and P------t, he owes his fame" (11. 79–80).[37]

Although, at least for the moment, Almon maintained his connection with Say,[38] he officially resigned from his position on the *Gazetteer* to start his own business. In the fall of 1763, Temple, along with other prominent Whigs, helped Almon establish himself at 178 Piccadilly (across from Burlington House), where Almon converted the ground floor of his dwelling into a bookshop.[39]

These years saw the wealthy politician and the ambitious bookseller working together for their mutual benefit. As Robert Rea so aptly put it, the "same press which made Temple a factor to be reckoned with in politics enabled John Almon to become a country gentleman."[40] This is partially because

Temple's chief delight was to stir up faction. Macaulay, with his characteristic lack of generosity, detailed Temple's operations:

> . . . those who knew his habits tracked him as men track a mole. It was his nature to grub underground. Whenever a heap of dirt was flung up, it might well be suspected that he was at work in some foul crooked labyrinth below.

Horace Walpole similarly described Temple as a "malignant man" who "worked in the *mines* of successive factions for nearly thirty years together."[41]

Since Temple increasingly had need of better access to the press, he found Almon especially attractive in terms of his early training, his grasp of politics and publishing, and his abilities as a writer and a businessman. Temple was quick to realize that Almon, a promising young man with exceptional talent, was ever on the lookout for patronage. And if Temple could provide Almon with significant subsidies and important connections, Almon could supply Temple with exactly what he most required, a powerful means of disseminating ideas. Contemporaries exhibited an extraordinary amount of interest in this relationship. For example, it was the subject of "A Curious Dialogue between a Certain Rt. Hon. Author and his Bookseller," which satirizes, among other things, Almon's formula for producing a tract.[42] In this attack, Almon, who is referred to at one point as "Little Vamp," is made to brag: "There is not a bookseller in London that knows better how to touch up an eighteen-penny pamphlet. I've always a collection of allegations, assertions, and ipsedixits, ready-made and well assorted, that will serve for any argument."

His patron responds: "—you'll be an alderman in two years,—and then may make every motion I want in the city."

Indeed, recognizing the extent to which Temple came to depend on Almon to help him obtain some of his most important political ends, Horace Walpole remarked, "Lord Temple just crawls about Almon's window in the shape of an autumnal fly that a child could crush. . . ."[43]

Of course, with the patronage of men like Temple came political pressure. One particularly striking example of the obligations this situation introduced occurred in 1766 after the falling-out between Chatham and Temple.[44] When Temple refused a place in the Pitt administration, Almon's hopes of office—at least for the time being—seemed to be over. Horace Walpole described this turn of events in his letter to Lord Holland of 19 July 1766:

> I SUPPOSE, my dear Lord, you will have had twenty letters by this post to tell you that Lord Temple has refused the Treasury and is gone. His creatures say Mr Pitt used him like a dog. I should not think that either was very gentle to the other before they parted. Lord Temple insisted on bringing his brother Geo. too, which Pitt refused. Then poor Lord Littleton; no. When all was rejected the Earl recollected Almon and Humphrey Cotes; not for lords of the Treasury, but as responsible to them. . . .[45]

Although Charles Townshend did, in fact, offer Almon a job in the newly formed Chatham administration, Almon felt compelled to reject it out of loyalty to Temple. On 20 August 1766 Almon gave Townshend his reply:

> It is not in language to describe the gratitude with which I am impressed by your last conversation. But it is my misfortune this year, as it was last year, to see my best friends differ. After the maturest considerations, pardon me, Sir, if I say that I cannot think of going to Stowe upon this subject. If Lord *Temple* consents, he must look coldly upon me ever afterwards; and if he refuses, it is putting him under an obligation to do something better whenever he comes into office. You know his lordship's temper; he is warm and decided; particularly at the present moment. I must therefore continue to lament in silence this unfortunate division, anxiously looking forward to better days. . . .[46]

Almon's letter to Temple of 15 July 1765 provides some evidence that his response here was influenced by an earlier experience, which left him suspicious of Townshend: ". . . I fear I have lost my supposed favour at the Pay Office, not having heard a word more about it, and it is near a fortnight since Mr. Townshend mentioned it, which makes many people think it a joke."[47] of course, in the present instance, Almon may have simply been waiting for a future offer (never to materialize) from Temple.[48]

From what little evidence we have of Almon's finances, it seems that, at least when it came to politics, his employers paid the printing expenses for material that Almon received free of charge.[49] In addition, most of these works came "prepaid"— that is, with extra money for unanticipated problems. Almon stood to make all the profit. Clearly, Almon's contemporaries understood how he was funded. For example, the matter-of-fact tone of the following description from the *Gentleman's Magazine* is of interest in and of itself because it may indicate that such arrangements were fairly common:

> With the manuscript of every pamphlet entrusted to his care an ample sum was deposited to defray all possible contingent expences; and the gain was exclusively his own.[50]

According to Horace Walpole, this gain was considerable. Walpole has it that Almon was eventually "reckoned to have made a fortune of £10,000 by publishing and selling libels."[51]

Situated so advantageously, Almon soon became London's chief Opposition publisher and his shop an important center for Opposition activity. Almon is said to have been unrivaled as the main Opposition bookseller of the second half of the eighteenth century. According to Lucyle Werkmeister, Almon's shop quickly became "the *locus operandi* for political activities generally."[52] Contemporary comment substantiates such claims. For instance, *Public Characters* (p. 128) describes Almon's shop as "the place of resort for the whole Opposition." And among the Almon papers preserved in the British Library is a letter in which Almon is referred to as "the favourite Publisher of Tracts on the Popular & Patriotic Side."[53]

In these circumstances it is small wonder that Almon's business increased significantly, as he began to publish works by important eighteenth-century figures such as Charles Townshend, Horace Walpole, Christopher Smart, Richard Grenville, George Grenville, William Knox, John Hall Stevenson, Charles Lloyd, and John Wilkes. (See appendix.) Within less than a year of establishing his own bookshop, Almon (through Temple's influence) was appointed official bookseller to the Coterie. This Whig club, which met at Wildman's tavern on Albermarle Street, was soon to become one of the most important of Opposition groups. John Brewer, who has described the company at Wildman's as "the most successful attempt at opposition organisation in the period," is quite right in characterizing Almon as "the club's press agent."[54] Since Almon was in this position in 1764, when several members of Wildman's decided to establish a party paper, it was natural enough that they approach him with the idea of conducting such a project. Although this never got beyond the planning stage, Almon did go so far as to urge Wilkes to serve as editor and to solicit contributions from Walpole.[55]

At the club's weekly dinners Almon could be found exchanging information and otherwise hobnobbing with the likes of Newcastle, Burke, Temple, Grafton, and Rockingham.[56] With such extensive political contacts as well as more significant friendships with Temple and Wilkes, Almon had good cause to congratulate himself. Almon's experiences in these early years would determine his future economic, political, and literary activities, his web of trade, and his network of relationships.

Notes

[1] *Memoirs*, pp. 9–12.
[2] *Memoirs*, pp. 9–12.
[3] *Memoirs*, pp. 12–13.
[4] *Memoirs*, p. 13.
[5] *Public Characters*, p. 121; Chalmers, p. 34; Ian Maxted, *The London Book Trades 1775–1800* (Kent: Dawson, 1977), p. 3.
[6] Add. MS. 20733 fo. 121.

12

[7] *Memoirs*, pp. 13.

[8] *The New Foundling Hospital for Wit*, ed. John Almon (1768–73; rpt. London: Debrett, 1786), III, 265.

[9] Add. MS. 20733 fos. 121–26.

[10] *Memoirs*, p. 13.

[11] Plomer, p. 265; *Public Characters*, p. 121. Williamson is best known for his *Liverpool Advertiser and Mercantile Chronicle*, which he published from its inception in 1756 until 1777 (Timperley, II, 696).

[12] Obituary, p. 1179.

[13] NYHS MS. fo. 34.

[14] *Memoirs*, p. 16n. The former Elizabeth Jackson of Milbank, Westminster was born on 25 December 1737 (John Almon, "Epitaph" in *The New Foundling Hospital for Wit*, III, 263). Although the Almons had ten children (*Memoirs*, p. 16), it is difficult to establish, with any degree of certainty, how many survived. References to Almon's children appear in *The New Foundling Hospital*, III, 268–69; John Almon, ed., *An Asylum for Fugitive Pieces* (1776–79; rpt. London: Printed for J. Debrett, 1785–95), pp. 58–61; Add. MS. 20733 fos. 4, 121, 127, 129; NYHS MS. fos. 29, 85, etc.

[15] These included *Gotham, The Ghost, Poems by C. Churchill, The Conference, The Author, The Duellist, The Candidate, The Farewell*, and *The Times*. A bibliography of Churchill's works may be found in Iolo Williams, *Seven Eighteenth-Century Bibliographies* (1924; rpt. New York: Burt Franklin, 1968). In addition, Almon published some of Wilkes's notes on Churchill's poems. See Almon's letter to Wilkes of 12 May 1767 (Add. MS 30869 fo. 123), *New Foundling Hospital for Wit*, III, 89–107, Almon's biography and letters of Wilkes, III, 5–84, and *Memoirs*, p. 41.

[16] Charles Ryskamp and John Baird, ed., *The Poems of William Cowper* (New York: Oxford University Press, 1980), I, xiii.

[17] *Public Characters*, p. 121; Chalmers, p. 34.

[18] Timperley, II, 822 and Maxted, p. 3. Watts (1678–1763) formerly patronized William Caslon and lent him money to start his great foundry. See *The Autobiography of Benjamin Franklin*, ed. Leonard Labaree, Ralph Ketcham, Helen Boatfield, and Helen Fineman (1791; rpt. New Haven: Yale University Press, 1964), p. 300.

[19] *Ibid.*, pp. 99–101; *Memoirs*, p. 14n.

[20] *Autobiography*, pp. 99–100.

[21] "Chapel" was the term for both the printing house and the organized body of journeymen printers in it. Headed by a senior member, each chapel wrote its own bylaws (*Ibid.*, p. 101).

[22] *Ibid.*, p. 101.

[23] Franklin was in England from 1724–26; 1757–62; 1764–75 (Chronology, *Autobiography*, pp. 303, 307, 309).

[24] Published by S. Fuller, Almon's analysis went through two editions. See *Public Characters*, pp. 121–22; Robert Watt, "Almon, John," *Bibliotheca Britannica* (1824); Alan Valentine, "Almon, John," *The British Establishment, 1760–1784* (1970); Alan Valentine, *Lord George Germain* (Oxford: The Clarendon Press, 1962), pp. 65–67; John Almon, *Biographical, Literary, and Political Anecdotes* (London: T.N. Longman and L.B. Seeley, 1797), II, 116–38.

Almon's next publication, *A New Military Dictionary* (London: J. Cooke, 1760), was essentially a compilation of battle descriptions from the reign of Charlemagne to 1760. In passing it should be noted that, curiously enough, around 1759 Almon may have written *London Courtship; or, A New Road to Matrimony. Consisting of Original Letters which Passed between a Celebrated Young Lady of the City of London and Several of her Suitors* (London: Printed for M. Thrush). See Andrew Block, *The English Novel 1740–1850: A Catalogue Including Prose Romances, Short Stories, and Translations of Foreign Fiction* (1939; rpt. New York: Oceana Publications, 1962), p. 143; National Union Catalogue.

[25] *Memoirs*, p. 14.

[26] *Public Characters*, p. 122.

[27] Haig argues that in 1762 Almon added two new features to the paper, "Articles of Literature and Entertainment" (summaries and extracts of other publications) and "Observations from our Correspondents" (a digest of letters received by the *Gazetteer*). Haig also suggests that Almon induced important Opposition politicians to contribute to the *Gazetteer*. See *The Gazetteer 1735–1797* (Carbondale: Southern Illinois University Press, 1960), pp. 51–54.

[28] Almon was to sign himself "Independent Whig" again when he criticized the government's handling of the war with America in his *Letter to the Right Honourable Charles Jenkinson* (London: Debrett, 1781), which ran through six editions. See entries 81-1a to 81-1f, 82-8, and 82-80 in Thomas R. Adams, *The American Controversy* (New York: Bibliographical Society of America, 1980), hereafter cited as *American Controversy*, and entry 40520 in Joseph Sabin and Wilberforce Eames, *Bibliotheca America* (New York: Printed for the Bibliographical Society of America, 1868–1936), hereafter cited as Sabin. Almon continued to use this pseudonym in his supplement to this popular tract, *An Address to the Interior Cabinet on the Affairs of America* (London: Debrett, 1782; Sabin 421; *American Controversy* 82-5a to 82-5c). Almon's further continuation of his *Letter, The Revolution in MDCCLXXXII Impartially Considered* (London: Debrett, 1782), which dealt with the change of ministry, was also signed "Independent Whig" (Sabin 70346; *American Controversy* 82-6a to 82-6b).

[29] Only a short time later (on Bute's resignation), Temple would assist Almon with his *Review of Lord Bute's Administration* (London: Printed for I. Pridden, 1763), which ran through three editions. Almon had previously traced the effects of ministerial influence in *A Review of the Reign of George the Second* (London: J. Wilkie, 1762), which ran through two editions the year it was published (Sabin 70256). Although the *Monthly Review* described this anonymous account as "a hasty performance; the matter ill digested," it pleased the Duke of Bedford so much that he (unsuccessfully) tried to discover the author. See "Monthly Catalogue," *The Monthly Review*, XXV (1762), 502 and *Public Characters*, p. 123.

In 1767 Almon would again take up the subject of Bute in *A Letter to the Earl of Bute, upon his Union with the Earl of Chatham, in Support of the Popular Measure of a Four-Shillings Land Tax* (London: J. Almon).

[30] *Memoirs*, pp. 14–15. To avoid confusion, at this point it should be noted that Almon wrote his *Memoirs* in the third person.

[31] Almon's *Review of Mr. Pitt's Administration*, which was published in London by Kearsly in 1762, ran through five editions and was translated into French and German. The following year saw the publication of *An Appendix to the Review of Mr. Pitt's Administration by the Author of the Review* (London: J. Almon, 1763).

Temple (1711–79) served as M.P. for Buckinghamshire before 1752, when he was created Earl Temple and succeeded to the House of Lords. In the same year he inherited the wealthy estates of Wotton and Stowe. Although Temple was appointed to several offices such as First Lord of the Admiralty and Lord Privy Seal, he is largely remembered as the active patron of Wilkes and the formidable opponent of Bute. For Almon's flattering outline of Temple's career, see his *Biographical . . . Anecdotes*, II, 1–64.

[32] One of Temple's last letters was addressed to Almon from Stowe on 24 August 1779. Speaking of himself (albeit in the third person), Temple wrote: "Lord Temple is much obliged to Mr. Almon for the interesting intelligence he has sent, is perfectly well in health, and not a little unhappy at the state of this country." Ironically enough, Temple died on 10 September 1779. See William James Smith, ed., *The Grenville Papers* (London: John Murray, 1853), IV, 575; *Memoirs*, p. 114.

[33] *Memoirs*, p. 32.

[34] Add. MS. 30868 fo. 136; *Memoirs*, p. 32. From the start, Almon appears to have known (and recorded) minute details of Temple's activities. Some idea of the nature of the information to which Almon had access is suggested by the many notes found among his papers in the New-York Historical Society. For example, on a scrap of paper dated 31 September 1763, Almon observed:

Ld Temple & Mr Pitt paid a visit to Mr Calcraft
Mr Pitt was 2 hours with the D of Cumberland who afterwards set out for Windsor as did Mr Pitt for Hayes & Ld Temple for Stowe (fo. 20).

[35] NYHS MS. fo. 84. On another occasion Almon similarly recalled with nostalgia the "former days in which I was honoured with peculiar mark of the gracious condescensions of the late earl [Temple] . . . when I lived in Picadilly" (Add. MS. 20733 fo. 1).

[36] Almon's personal letters to Newcastle are located in the British Library, Add. MSS. 32939 (fo. 242), 32959 (fo. 233), and 33069 (fo. 233).

[37] Henry Dell, as cited by Terry Belanger, "A Directory of the London Book Trade, 1766," *Publishing History*, I (1977), 16. Belanger—correctly, I think—supplies "Wilkes" and "Pitt".

[38] Haig (p. 55) speculates that Almon contributed a series of letters entitled "The Contrast," which appeared in the *Gazetteer* through the summer of 1765.

[39] *Memoirs*, p. 16; Haig, pp. 55 and 88; Maxted, p. 3. In passing it should be mentioned that the Almon collection at the New-York Historical Society (fo. 81) includes a rent receipt made out in the amount of ten pounds for three months. It is dated 18 April 1769 and endorsed by Thomas Turner.

[40] *The English Press in Politics 1760–1774* (Lincoln: University of Nebraska Press, 1963), p. 91.

[41] *Memoirs of the Reign of King George the Third*, ed. G.F. Russell Barker (1822; rpt. New York: G.P. Putnam's Sons, 1894), II, 359.

[42] This anonymous piece was prefixed to *A Letter to the Right Honourable the Earl of Temple* (1763; rpt. London: S. Bladon, 1766).

[43] Horace Walpole to Lord Holland, 14 November 1766 in W.S. Lewis and Robert A. Smith, ed. *Horace Walpole's Correspondence* (New Haven: Yale University Press, 1961), XXX, 237. Walpole is referring here to *An Enquiry into the Conduct of a Late Right Honourable Commoner*, which was displayed in the window of Almon's shop in Piccadilly. (See below.)

[44] In July of 1766, Pitt (now Chatham) took office again, replacing the Rockingham administration. However close Pitt and Temple had been when Almon first met them, by this time they were at odds. (For one thing, Temple supported the position on America taken by George Grenville, his brother.) Temple's version of his quarrel with

Pitt may be found in *An Enquiry into the Conduct of a Late Right Honourable Commoner* (London: Printed for J. Almon, 1766). This pamphlet, which was written by Humphrey Cotes and Almon at Temple's behest, contains details of private conversations that could only have been supplied by Temple (Lewis and Smith, ed., XXX, 225n).

[45] Lewis and Smith ed., XXX, 225–26. According to the Yale editors, Walpole's account, while representative of reports in general circulation, was inaccurate: It seems that Temple and Pitt never discussed the specific appointments mentioned in this letter. See John Brooke, *The Chatham Administration 1766–1768* (New York: St. Martin's Press, 1956), p. 8.

[46] *Memoirs*, p. 34. For Almon's poem on the change of ministry in 1766, "The Congratulation," see *Asylum for Fugitive Pieces*, pp. 62–63.

[47] *Grenville Papers*, III, 49. Almon's poem "A Sketch," which deals with the change of ministry in 1765, may be found in *New Foundling Hospital for Wit*, III, 258–59.

[48] In his *Memoirs* Almon registered a previous disappointment:

> Had the negociation for a change of ministers succeeded, in the autumn of 1763, Lord *Temple*, who was to have been at the head of the Treasury, had designed Mr. *Almon* for a situation. It was an irreparable loss to Mr. Almon, as well as to some others of Lord *Temple's* friends, that his lordship never chose to accept any of the many offers which were made to him by the court (p. 32).

[49] Chalmers, p. 35.

[50] Obituary, p. 1179. Some variation of this system seems to have extended to almost all of Almon's business dealings. For example, consider the terms of the following letter dated 16 April 1775 from a T.P. Andrews, Esq., proposing that Almon publish *A Letter to James Macpherson, Esq*, which appeared under the pseudonym "Rustic" later that year:

> The Author of the inclosed Work addresses himself to Mr Almon. . . . He desires him to print the inclosed Pamphlet. . . . The Author is in no way anxious as to the Profit. . . . He apprehends that it will make a Shilling Quarto. . . . He apprehends that the expence of printing, Paper &c will be about Five Pounds, & the Advertisements, Three or Four Pounds more—A Hazard which he himself will run, unless Mr Almon should chose to make him some Offer for the Copy. The Author would have five hundred Copies printed. . . . He desires to have the Proof Sheets sent down to him as fast as they are done that he may correct them (Add. MS. 20733 fo. 6).

See also *Memoirs*, p, 92, where a similar arrangement is proposed. On occasion, however, Almon appears to have provided some financial backing. (See Add. MS. 30868 fo. 136, 38728 fo. 194, 38730 fo. 10, and below, chapter 5.)

[51] *Memoirs of the Reign of King George the Third*, IV, 106. Walpole, who had no high opinion of Almon, suggested, "Everybody must live by their trade; abuse was Almon's trade" (III,83).

[52] *The London Daily Press, 1772–1797* (Lincoln: University of Nebraska Press, 1963), pp. 111–12.

[53] Add. MS. 20733 fo. 6.

[54] *Party Ideology and Popular Politics at the Accession of George III* (New York: Cambridge University Press, 1976), pp. 60–61. See also D.H. Watson, "The Rise of the Opposition at Wildman's," *Bulletin of the Institute of Historical Research*, XLIV (1971), 57–77.

[55] Add. MS. 30868 fos. 136–37; *The Grenville Papers*, II, 457–58; Brewer, pp. 227–28.

[56] Almon included a list of club members in *The History of the Late Minority* (1765; rpt. London: n.p., 1766), pp. 297–300. Although Watt attributes this work to Almon alone, it has also been attributed to both Almon and Temple. See *Grenville Papers*, p. 248 and Carl Cone, *Burke and the Nature of Politics* (Lexington: University of Kentucky Press, 1957), pp. 60–61. For Wilkes's temporary quarrel with Almon over *The History*, see Biography and letters, III, 135 and Robert Rea, "Bookseller as Historian," *The Indiana Quarterly for Bookmen*, V (1949), 79. (Wilkes's copy of Almon's work with his extensive marginalia is located in the British Library.) Almon's poem "To the Late Minority: Written on Reading the History of their Conduct, Entitled 'An History of the Late Minority,' &c." may be found in *The New Foundling Hospital for Wit*, III, 259–61.

Around this time Almon wrote several other political works. Watt attributes *An Impartial History of the Late War* (London: Printed for J. Johnson, 1763) to Almon. The year 1764 saw the publication of Almon's *An History of the Parliament of Great Britain from the Death of Queen Anne to the Death of King George II* (London: Printed for G. Kearsly). In addition, *A Parallel between the Siege of Berwick and the Siege of Aquilea* is attributed to Almon by *Public Characters* (p. 135), by Chalmers (p. 35), and by Watt. This last work is an attack on John Home's *The Siege of Aquilea*.

17

2
John Almon and
John Wilkes

Robert Rea's article "John Almon: Bookseller to John Wilkes"
examines Almon and Wilkes's negotiation for Wilkes's *History
of England from the Revolution*, their falling-out over Almon's
History of the Late Minority, and their fear of political reprisals for
Almon's publication of Wilkes's *Letter to his Grace the Duke of
Grafton*.[1] In a second article Rea describes the last part of
Almon's career with particular reference to his *Anecdotes of . . .
Pitt* and his edition of Wilkes and of Junius.[2]

All this is well enough—as far as it goes. While studies of this
kind can help us to account for the circumstances attending the
publication of these works, they do not altogether explore the
extent of Almon's association with Wilkes. After all, the two
were the best of friends for thirty-six years, until Wilkes's death
in 1797. Almon insisted that over these years "no material
circumstances occurred in the condition of either that was not
mutually known."[3] To analyze the relationship between
Almon and Wilkes more closely, in this chapter I will do three
things: First, I will examine Almon's participation in the affair
of Number 45 of the *North Briton* and his early activities on
behalf of Wilkes. Next, I will consider Almon's efforts to keep
Wilkes well informed in matters of English politics after he had
fled to France. And finally I will take up Almon's part in
Wilkes's media campaign during his years in exile.

From the very beginning, Almon's friendship with Wilkes
was put to the test. In fact, Almon was destined to witness and
chronicle events surrounding Wilkes's arrest for his part in

producing the *North Briton*, Number 45. Some idea of Almon's involvement can be obtained by examining his most interesting eyewitness report, which appears, appropriately enough, in his biography of Wilkes.[4] Here Almon begins with a discussion of what precipitated Number 45.

According to Almon, on the evening of 18 April 1763, Temple and Pitt had the opportunity to read an advance copy of the speech the King would deliver the following day. At the same time, Wilkes chanced to arrive at Temple's house in Pall Mall. All three had serious objections to the speech, and their discussion formed the basis of the celebrated Number 45 of the *North Briton*, which was issued on 23 April 1763.[5]

Since there was no doubt that this attack could be classified as a seditious libel, Lords Halifax and Egremont, the two Secretaries of State, moved quickly to prosecute those involved with its production. Among the first to be apprehended were the publisher and printer, who named Wilkes (by this time, Member of Parliament for Aylesbury) as the editor of Number 45.[6]

In describing Wilkes's arrest, Almon tells us a good deal about his own efforts to aid his friend. On the morning of 30 April Almon arrived at Wilkes's house shortly after three messengers had arrested Wilkes on a general warrant—that is, a warrant that specified the offense but not the offender(s).[7] According to Almon, his timing was purely coincidental. He says he "happened to call on Mr. Wilkes, not from any knowledge of the circumstance, but because he had for some time been in the habit of occasionally visiting that gentleman."[8] Although Charles Churchill entered the scene a short time later, he departed immediately when Wilkes warned him by addressing him as Mr. Thompson and inquiring, "How does Mrs. Thompson today? Does she dine in the country?"[9]

Allowed to step into Wilkes's parlor, Almon found him deeply engaged in conversation with the messengers. Wilkes quickly spied Almon and pulled him aside. Obviously eager to acquaint Almon with the details of his situation, Wilkes drew him to the other end of the room. As he rapidly whispered his

20

circumstances to Almon, it became apparent that Wilkes would need a writ of *habeas corpus* to bring him before a court. Wilkes frantically appealed to Almon, pleading for him to alert Temple immediately.

Much to his astonishment, Almon was not prevented from leaving the house. *Public Characters* reported:

> The messengers did not detain Mr. Almon, which they might have done; and for which negligence they were very much blamed by Lord Halifax, because it gave rise to another circumstance which was of great importance. Mr. Almon immediately informed Earl Temple of Mr. Wilkes's situation. . .(p. 125).[10]

Upon learning of Wilkes's predicament, Temple instructed Almon to contact Arthur Beardmore, Temple's attorney, at once. As Robert Rea puts it, in so doing, Almon "first set in motion the legal action which ended in Wilkes's triumphant release from the tower and the clutches of a general warrant."[11]

When Wilkes's case came to trial on 3 May 1763, the prosecution had little difficulty in establishing that Number 45 was a libel. The actual focus of this case was the legality of general warrants.[12] Because he was the first vigorously to challenge the issuing of general warrants, a procedure that had long been prevalent, Wilkes became an overnight sensation.[13] It is true that the case against Wilkes was dismissed because of his privilege as a Member of Parliament; nevertheless, he drew attention to a problem that would finally be resolved some years later when general warrants were held to be illegal in the case of *Entick* v. *Carrington* (1765) and in a House of Commons declaration (1766).[14]

Although the legal principles involved here are quite important, since the object of this chapter is to examine Almon's relationship with Wilkes, what is of interest at this point is Almon's publishing activity on behalf of his friend. During this difficult time, Almon supported Wilkes by publishing *A Letter to Kidgell* and *A Letter Concerning Libels*.

Before discussing the first of these pamphlets, however, some background information would seem to be in order. Despite Temple's strenuous efforts to dissuade him, Wilkes had set up his own printing press only a few short weeks after his release from the Tower. Almon says he was present at one interview where he

> heard lord Temple assure Mr. Wilkes that he (Wilkes) could not name any sum of money which his lordship would not be ready to advance, if Mr. Wilkes would remove the printing-press; but he was obstinate, and would yield to no entreaty.[15]

Had Wilkes been content with his acquittal, he might have been able to avoid further legal repercussions. But instead, he used his private press to reprint his *North Briton* and to print—albeit solely for private enjoyment—a dozen copies of the first part of *An Essay on Woman*, which is generally attributed to Thomas Potter.[16] According to Almon, Potter "was the worst; and was indeed the ruin of Mr. Wilkes, who was not a bad man early, or naturally. But Potter poisoned his morals."[17]

By its very nature, Potter's pornographic take-off on Pope was difficult to defend. Unfortunately, the government obtained a copy of the parody and again initiated proceedings against Wilkes. This time Wilkes was charged not only with seditious libel for reprinting Number 45, but also with obscene libel for printing *An Essay on Woman*. Wilkes's position was a delicate one, and—whatever may be thought of the poem—Almon deserves credit for defending his friend. Almon's support took the form of his tract, *A Letter to Kidgell*, written in response to the Reverend J. Kidgell's pamphlet attack on Wilkes's poem.[18] Here Almon charged that by publishing extracts of *An Essay on Woman* in his criticism of Wilkes, Kidgell made public a work judged to be obscene but intended for a private audience only.

Not surprisingly, Wilkes was convicted of both charges of libel. When he failed to appear to receive his sentence because he had been wounded in a duel, Wilkes was expelled and declared an outlaw. It was at this point (in late December of 1763) that Wilkes fled to France. Shortly thereafter Almon published *A Letter Concerning Libels*, which, in its consideration of Wilkes's trial, attacked Lord Mansfield and involved Almon in a law suit of his own.[19]

There has been much conjecture about "Father of Candor," the pseudonymous author of *A Letter Concerning Libels*. *The Gentleman's Magazine* attributed it to Chief Justice Pratt (afterwards, Lord Camden); Horace Walpole attributed it to John Dunning (afterwards, Lord Ashburton), and Almon himself attributed it to both Pratt and Dunning.[20] In any event, it was John Almon who, as publisher of the tract, was prosecuted for libel at Lord Mansfield's request. And it is this trial that marks the beginning of Almon's legal difficulties.

The political basis of Almon's trial was apparent. One reason for his prosecution was that the pamphlet attack on the administration contained lengthy arguments about two of the most controversial issues of the time. "Father of Candor's" particular targets were the legality of general warrants and the notion of libel as set out by Lord Mansfield, the Chief Justice. (See below.) The tract also called into question Mansfield's alteration of a passage in the record of Wilkes's trial.[21]

After a slight delay, Almon's trial began on 1 May 1765 in the Court of King's Bench. On the grounds that he was an interested party, Lord Mansfield temporarily stepped down, leaving Sir John Eardley Wilmot to preside in his place.[22] As in Wilkes's trial, at least at the outset, the point at issue was the mode of proceeding.[23] Instead of being tried by indictment or information,[24] as was usual in cases of libel, Almon was tried by attachment—that is, without a jury. It seems fair to assume, with the defense, that it was prejudicial to dispense with the jury when Almon was tried before Lord Mansfield's colleagues. Under these conditions, the chief objection urged by the counsel for Almon was that a writ of attachment was inappropriate in the case of libel on the Court or a judge acting in his official capacity. The defense, in effect, argued that "if the attachment goes, the court exercises the distinct and peculiar provinces of party, judge, evidence, and jury."[25]

Due to a technicality, Almon's trial dragged on and was delayed, never to progress beyond the fundamental question of procedure.[26] It says much for Almon's connections that in July, 1765, when the administration changed and Rockingham took office, charges against Almon were dropped.[27] Perhaps Almon was more fortunate than he knew. Wilmot's undelivered judgment (first published in 1802) was approved by his fellow judges. It held that the Court had the right to punish libels on itself by attachment.[28]

Almon's other efforts on behalf of Wilkes when he was abroad were considerable. To begin with, Wilkes made constant demands on Almon for information. At the same time, he insisted that the nature of their letters remain confidential. On 30 April 1767, for instance, Wilkes wrote Almon:

> Pray, write me all the news; but never mention that we are correspondents, except as to sending me books. . . . The most minute things are interesting to us here, at so great a distance. You may depend upon my secrecy, and pray do not omit any thing curious.[29]

Wilkes made a similar request on 11 May 1767, when he repeated that the only connection with Almon that he would publicly acknowledge was professional: "Pray send me minutely all the news; and all the chit-chat of London, respecting the great folks. I will never shew your letters to any one, nor even say I have heard from you but as a bookseller."[30]

Corresponding with Wilkes was obviously not without its problems. Both Almon and Wilkes frequently mentioned the fear that their letters would be intercepted by the post office. In fact, they often devised schemes to elude detection. For example, on 23 October 1764, Almon took the precaution of forwarding his letter to Wilkes by way of a travelling friend:

I take the opportunity of writing by M^r [Humphrey] Coates as I know this will be put *safe* into your hands. My letters by the post I have reason to think miscarried. You mentioned the receipt of only *one* whereas I wrote *four*. Your *last* letter to me mentioned the sending of something particular in a former letter. Whatever that *something partic-ular* was it never came to hand.[31]

On 14 April 1767, Almon instructed Wilkes:

Whenever you chuse to write per post direct thus (without any inside cover) *To Mrs Mary Jackson to be left at Mr Tuke's, Distiller, in Fleet Street, London*; which I think will sufficiently elude the suspicious & imperti-nent curiosity of persons in office.[32]

Almon sent Wilkes the same forwarding instructions on 30 April 1767.[33] And on 12 May 1767 Almon provided Wilkes with three different addresses to deceive as well as to test the post office:

Private hands if they are honest are the best channels of conveyance, for neither property nor secrets are safe on this side the water from the theft or inspection of the Minister or his agents. The post office constantly affords a most horrid scene of infamy or it is much belied. However as for expedition's sake you say the post office is the best conveyance. I have contrived 3 directions lest letters coming continu-ally to one place might at length afford suspicion.
They are
1. To Mrs Jackson at Mr Tuke's distiller in Fleet Street
2. To Mrs Jackson Church Street St John's Westminster
3. To Mr Abraham Long to be left at Mr Bladon's in Pater Noster Row
And if you will take the trouble of directing your first second & third letters in the above manner beginning again with the first direction for your fourth letter & so on I shall know whether there has been any trick or mistake in the delivery of any of them.[34]

Despite all these obstacles, Almon's desire to provide his friend with accurate information brought him into close corre-spondence with Wilkes. Almon's letters to Wilkes lie, for the most part neglected, among the Wilkes papers in the British Library. Forming part of a large collection, they date primarily

25

from the late sixties. During this time Almon had much to do in the way of keeping Wilkes well informed about Temple in particular and about political changes in general.

Almon's letter to Wilkes of 23 October 1764 is to my knowledge the first of his many attempts to assess Temple's attitude toward Wilkes:

> Lord Temple who I know you esteem as the honestest man in the whole party is the same good Lord that he used to be. I saw him about two months ago at Stowe & you of course was the subject of part of our conversation. He said then as he said all last winter that your case if it had been properly managed would infallibly have broke the necks of the administration. The whole public say so & I assure you the minority have received no small injury in the opinion of the people by so scandalously neglecting it.[35]

Wilkes's letter to Almon of 30 April 1767 reflects what were to become frequent inquiries about their common patron. Here Wilkes asked about the state of affairs between Temple and James Grenville.[36] In Almon's reply, which is dated 12 May 1767, he reported that the two were at odds: "Mr James Grenville and his Lordship [Temple] have differed: They do not even visit."[37] In the same letter Almon reassured Wilkes of Temple's continued friendship: "I had very lately some conversation with his lordship concerning you. You may depend upon it he is still your friend."

Almon's next letter to Wilkes is among his harshest statements. It informs Wilkes of Temple's reaction to the publication of Wilkes's letter concerning the Talbot affair. A remark ridiculing Lord Talbot, a hot young government supporter, had appeared in the *North Briton* on 21 August 1762, whereupon Talbot confronted Wilkes, demanding to know if he was the author of the insult. When Wilkes repeatedly refused to answer, the two arranged a duel. Although immediately before the showdown was to take place, Talbot did everything short of withdrawing, one shot was finally exchanged. The duel ended as a draw. Talbot, however, came out of this incident seeming even more the fool: Wilkes had detailed Talbot's pre-duel hysteria at length in a letter to Temple. Much to Talbot's mortification, Wilkes later saw to it that this letter was published. Talbot assumed—incorrectly—that this was done at Temple's behest. Although Talbot's accusations made Temple furious enough to contemplate dueling with Talbot himself, he was angry at Wilkes for humiliating Talbot at the very time Talbot was voting with the Opposition.[38] It fell to Almon to rebuke Wilkes.[39] In his letter of 3 July 1767, Almon began by specifying how Wilkes's actions had affected him personally. It seems that although Almon had been provided with a copy of Wilkes's letter, he had sensed the impropriety of printing it. He therefore held off inserting it in his *Political Register*[40] until he was taken by surprise when a copy appeared in the *St. James's Chronicle*:

I am sorry you have blamed me about some late particulars but be assured I will never hurt you willfully. Your letter to lord Temple concerning the Battle of Bagshot did you incredible harm. Your best friends disapproved of that Publication. It was given to me 3 months ago for the first No. of the Political Register but I did not chuse to print it & your brother knows it & my reasons: at the same time or a very few days after my saying so over came your packet by Mr Spooner inclosing another for the printer of the S^t. James's Chronicle: I sent it of course not knowing the contents which if I had, I honestly confess I would have burnt. 2 days afterwards the letter appeared in that paper & the printer told me & everybody else that he received it from you along with a copy of your letter to the Duke of Grafton. Then I could do no less then reprint it in the Register.[41]

Almon went on to describe Temple's reaction:

Lord Talbot sent to Lord Temple to know if he authorised the Publication of that letter; lord Temple answered that he did not. Next day lord Talbot asked lord Temple in the Prince's Chamber if he avowed that Publication. lord Temple declared upon his honour that he did not (& by the bye he was very much vex'd at it for lord Talbot had lately been several times in the Minority) but that you sent it to him & afterwards at your own request had it back. This authenticated the letter, & made lord Talbot more angry: he then insisted that lord Temple should give it him under his hand that he did not authorize that

Publication. Lord Temple replied *not by compulsion*. lord Talbot then called out lord Gower & lord Harcourt & asked them if his demand was not reasonable? they said no. Still he was not satisfied & swore he would fight lord Temple: the latter said with all his heart & actually drew his sword. The other lords prevented any thing further, except lord Temple's declaration he was ready to fight lord Talbot at any time or place.[42]

Not only did Almon relate Temple's feelings and activities, but, more generally, he enabled Wilkes to keep track of the vicissitudes of English politics. For one thing, Almon was directly involved with insuring that Wilkes received current political literature. More often than not, Almon's letters written during this period refer to the pamphlets, journals, and newspapers he regularly sent Wilkes.[43] On numerous occasions Wilkes gratefully acknowledged the receipt of this material.[44] Of course, Almon forwarded many pieces with which he was in some way associated. On 15 March 1767, for instance, Almon assured Wilkes "What I print you shall always have."[45] These productions Almon seems to have supplied free of charge.[46]

Naturally enough, Almon was quick to report developments that he thought might affect Wilkes's status. This, of course, included possible ministerial changes—especially important from the point of view of Wilkes. For example, Almon's letter to Wilkes of 20 July 1767 contained an up-to-the-minute record of potential changes in government. Almon (as it turned out, wrongly) advised Wilkes that everything was pointing to a Rockingham administration:

A negotiation for a Change of Ministers is on foot. The following particulars you may safely depend upon. About the 4th inst: the K. [ing] sent a letter to lord Chatham (who is ill at Hempstead) desiring his advice in the Choice of a new set of servants: Lord Chatham returned only a verbal answer to this effect "that such was his ill state of health his M. [ajesty] must not expect any advice whatever from him nor any assistance in any arrangement whatever." On the 5th (Sunday) lord B. [ute] was with the K. all day at Richmond. On the 9th the K. employed the Duke of G[rafton] to apply to lord Rockingham to form a new administration (You will observe, by the way, that of all the Opposition lord R. is considered as the *least* hostile to lord B.) Lord R. made answer that he would consult the Duke of Bedford: & he went to Wooburn. The Duke of B. said he would not do any thing without consulting lord Temple & Mʳ Grenville. Mʳ Rigby went to them. Their answer was, that as the K. had thought proper to treat with lord R. they would not take any places but if their friends were provided for they would support his lordship's administration; & in like manner they would have expected the same relinquishing from his lordship for himself personally, had the K. thought proper to have treated with them; & would have offered him the same condition for his friends. The Duke of B. said the same: that he would take no place, but desired that his friends might be provided for. The Duke of Newcastle has also relinquished for himself but made the same condition for his friends. Last Thursday lord R. gave his answer to the Duke of G. that he was ready to undertake the K.'s administration upon a broad & *comprehensive* system including the friends of every party. The K. on Friday agreed to the proposal: but under the description of comprehension he directly included his own friends (ie Bute's) & those about his person. Tomorrow lord R. is to have his audience.—Lord R. is to be first lord of the Treasury. The above is at present all that is certain. I could add a thousand Reports; but they are all conjectures: The above is very exact & impartial. . . .[47]

Since it seemed that, in all likelihood, these late developments would affect Wilkes's situation, Almon offered to intercede on his behalf: "Would you have me if the above change takes place say anything to lord T[emple] or Mʳ Fitzherbert concerning yourself you may entirely command and depend upon me."[48]

Under these circumstances, it was not long before Wilkes replied. In his letter to Almon of 30 July 1767 Wilkes outlined the implications for himself of the proposed changes:

If the political change you mention takes place, I should naturally imagine that the very idea of a "general comprehensive system" must include me, my pardon, my return, an indemnity, &c. . . . I will write to Mr. Fitzherbert as soon as I find the arrangement you mention takes place. I hope that I shall not be forgot, though so long absent.[49]

Ironically, at the time this letter was written, Almon's letter informing Wilkes that Rockingham had been unable to form a

29

government had already been sent. On 29 July 1767 Almon
wrote:

> My last brought the negotiation for a change of ministers to lord
> Rockingham's sending for the Duke of Bedford to town. His Grace
> came, in consequence of that request, on the 19th instant; & the next
> day there was a meeting at Newcastle House in Lincoln's Inn Fields to
> settle the arrangement of men. There were present the dukes of
> Newcastle Bedford Portland & Richmond Marquis of Rockingham Earl
> of Sandwich adm. Keppel Mr Rigby & Mr Dowdeswell: when lord
> Rockingham proposed himself for the Treasury & Mr Dowdeswell for
> his chancellor of the Exchequer to both which the Duke of Bedford
> agreed. Lord Rockingham then proposed Mr Conway for Secretary of
> State for the Southern department & minister of the House of Com-
> mons to which the duke of Bedford would not consent. His Grace said
> the military was Mr Conway's proper line: he had not the least
> objection to his being provided for in that establishment . . . Lord
> Rockingham would not recede from his proposal nor would the Duke
> of Bedford agree to it. The Conference therefore broke off on Wednes-
> day Lord Rockingham told the King he had no plan of administration
> to lay before him. His lordship is since gone to Yorkshire I have taken
> down all the particulars of this . . . negotiation & the whole conversa-
> tion at the Conference from the mouth of one of the persons present &
> I assure the whole is very much to lord Rockingham's dishonour.
> Friends as well as enemies blame him exceedingly. Nobody has the
> least guess what will next be done. . . .[50]

On 29 August 1767 Almon updated and continued his
account of changes in the administration:

> As to the News the Political Register will give you a good deal. But I
> must add that this week another Negotiation for a Change of minister
> is begun. I am not yet informed of the particulars. But it is with the D.
> of Bedford: who is come to town. Lord Rockingham you will see by the
> account has foolishly thrown the game out of his own hands: & the
> present ministry are not strong enough to stand; & if they were, they
> would be ruined by the continual disagreements amongst themselves.
> If a new administration is formed the parliament will certainly be
> dissolved: You may depend upon it. The reason is obvious: it is not
> worth any body's while to vacate his seat & the general Election so
> near. If anything comes of this fresh attempt to Change I shall send you
> advice of it.[51]

30

Other letters wherein Almon sent Wilkes vital political information could, of course, be cited. They are of great general interest; however, enough has been said to indicate that when Wilkes was living in France, Almon was concerned to provide him with minute details about Temple and about fluctuations in the English political scene. In any event, a further and perhaps more important point needs to be made in an analysis of the related careers of Almon and Wilkes: While Wilkes was abroad, Almon made sure that he was not forgotten at home.

Shrewd businessman that he was, Almon no doubt realized that, by its very nature, any publication by Wilkes was potentially profitable. Beyond this, however, the most compelling reason for Wilkes to remain the focus of attention was that he needed public support to obtain a pardon.[52] And Almon clearly recognized that unless Wilkes capitalized on his popularity by writing from abroad, he would be quickly forgotten. In his letter of 23 October 1764, the earliest of Almon's surviving letters to Wilkes, Almon urged him to write a comprehensive critique of the administration in the case of Number 45. Almon reasoned that such a project would help maintain the interest of the public in his cause:

I since mentioned it to your brother & he agreed with me in thinking that nothing would do so much service to your cause *by keeping it properly alive* & properly understood & preserving the affections of the people who you know are too apt to forget things if not seasonally reminded of them.[53]

When assessing Almon's role in this respect, it is necessary to consider two related factors in particular: Almon's *Political Register*, which was, in the main, a vehicle for Wilkite propaganda, and his preparations for Wilkes's return to England.

In April of 1767, Almon informed Wilkes of his plan to publish what would become the *Political Register* and went on to solicit contributions: "If you would be so obliging to furnish me with any thing for it, you would thereby do me a particular &

essential service."[54] In his next letter, after again requesting Wilkes's help on his new venture, Almon remarked, "You see I go all lengths in the cause of liberty."[55]

In May, 1767 Almon issued the first number of his *Political Register*, a politically oriented monthly periodical, which Chalmers characterized as "the general receptacle of all the scurrility of the writers in opposition to government" (p. 34).[56]

Wilkes enthusiastically offered his assistance in a letter dated 11 May 1767.[57] And on 12 June, shortly after the publication of the first issues, which he had forwarded, Almon provided a description of his new project:

> I sent you (by the Dover postage) two of the *Political Registers*, the moment it was published, & which I hope you have received. I think it will not displease you: & I assure you it will be carried on with spirit and in support of the true cause of Liberty. . . . You see the nature of the Plan. A miscellany of politics: And a Review of Books. An account of any Interesting & valuable foreign Book will be acceptable. . . .[58]

From the start Almon wrote Wilkes that the *Political Register* "is always at your service."[59] Indeed, according to John Brewer, the *Political Register* was one of the main publications that served as a mouthpiece for Wilkes and his supporters: "Almon's *Political Register* and the . . . *Freeholders Magazine* were virtually Wilkite organs."[60] Items in Almon's journal regularly promoted Wilkes's cause, hinting that he would return to England to run in the general election. Wilkes, of course, figured as one of Almon's chief contributors. In his letters he constantly referred to copy that he had sent Almon.[61] In turn, Almon's letters frequently acknowledged the receipt of Wilkes's material.[62]

The *Political Register* scored an instant success. Only five months after his journal was launched, Almon was pleased to observe: "The Political Register succeeds beyond my most sanguine expectations. It is become the fashionable political publication of the times."[63]

One matter remains to be discussed as having a bearing on the relationship between Almon and Wilkes at this time: During Wilkes's exile, Almon helped him deal with perhaps his most pressing dilemma, preparing for his reception in England.[64] My consideration of Almon's contribution here will focus primarily on Wilkes's *Letter to his Grace the Duke of Grafton*. In the interest of clarity, however, it seems best to begin with the political context of this publication.

In May, 1766, after having lived abroad for two years, Wilkes returned to England, where he had been charged in 1763 with publishing Number 45 and *An Essay on Woman*. Since by this time the Whigs had been returned to power, Wilkes expected to receive a pardon as well as political patronage. When neither was forthcoming, he returned to France. Several months later, he was encouraged to travel to London again, this time to seek Grafton's aid in dealing with Chatham. Grafton, however, ignored him and, disappointed a second time, Wilkes returned to Paris.[65] Having twice failed to obtain a pardon and finding himself regarded with ambivalence or apathy on almost every side, Wilkes now turned to journalists like Almon to help create a receptive climate for his return.

Seldom has anyone so wholeheartedly promoted himself as Wilkes. Of course, Wilkes's success was only possible with wide access to the press. And effective use of the press was Wilkes's particular strength. Wilkes's media blitz made him an instant hero, not the less so for his flashy style. John Brewer has analyzed Wilkes's strategy at this point:

Wilkes had . . . to sustain interest in his cause, and the only means at his disposal to achieve this was the press. . . . In his absence interest in him has naturally waned. . . . Taking stock of his difficulties, Wilkes realised that he was defeating his own ends by trying to return to England as discreetly as possible. Only if he returned with a fanfare of publicity would he be able to extricate himself from his political and financial difficulties. He therefore set out to prepare the ground for his return by launching a private press campaign on his own behalf. . . .[66]

This time when he went back to France, Wilkes immediately started his media campaign with his *Letter to his Grace the Duke of Grafton*, a work that Brewer has quite aptly described as the "opening salvo" in Wilkes's attempt to reestablish himself at the forefront of English politics.[67]

Although several papers printed extracts, Almon published a fuller (though by no means complete) version, which placed him in considerable danger of prosecution. This is apparent in his letter to Wilkes of 9 May 1767:

> The Public papers inserted as much [of the *Letter to . . . Grafton*] as they durst. . . . I have indeed printed more of it than any of them for which it is not certain whether I am yet in danger of the House as it has been much talked of there today.[68]

Almon described his situation in much the same terms several days later:

> Give me leave to remark that your spirited letter to the D. [uke] of G. [rafton] would never have been read by one 40th part of the persons who now almost adore it & you if it had not been reprinted. And would you have deemed me in my senses if I had reprinted it verbatim et literatim from your copy? Certainly not. And yet castrated even as it was I was in real danger of a commitment by the Ho: [House] of Com: [Commons]—if one word (not a name) more had been inserted, I had not escaped. And where is the party after the treachery so remarkable in your cause the infamous usage you have received & the scandalous desertion I have experienced that is worth running a risk for? Sir there are not 5 men in the Kingdom I would go across the way to serve.[69]

Wilkes clearly recognized Almon's risk in publishing his expanded account, however "castrated" it may have been. Accordingly, he expressed his concern for Almon's safety in his letter of 11 May 1767, which reads in part as follows:

> I am glad that the public approve my letter to the duke of Grafton. . . .
> Is it necessary in all cases, that your name should be in the title-page?
> Cannot you, for your own safety, reprint a thing without your name in

the title-page, and get it sold by underlings and hawkers, whom it would be ridiculous to take up and prosecute? You should think of some such scheme, for at present you run great risks.

I think the speaker cannot lay hold of you, as there are not even the initials of his name. The house of lords are more dangerous. They are more tender; though not more sore, nor rotten. I am at your service, to do what you will here in the cause of liberty.[70]

Although Almon strenuously exerted himself on behalf of Wilkes both when he was in exile and upon his return to England in 1768, throughout this period Almon was intermittently ill. At least as early as his letter to Wilkes of 15 March 1767, Almon referred to his "severe illness" and described himself as "[w]ith the assistance of our good friend Dr Brocklesby . . . just able to crawl downstairs and a little about."[71] Almon ended this letter by apologizing for being forced to leave off because he found himself "too weak with writing these few lines to say more. . . ." Within several weeks, however, Almon recovered, as Wilkes's flattering letter to Almon of 7 April 1767 indicates:

I heartily congratulate you on your recovery; and I desire you to thank Dr. Brocklesby from me, for the services he has done in restoring so good a friend to liberty.[72]

Since Almon and John Calcraft regularly exchanged letters about their various indispositions, their correspondence can serve as a valuable index of Almon's health during this time.[73] Both men thought they suffered from gout. For example, in a holograph draft of a letter to Calcraft dated 22 February 1772, Almon reported on his condition:

. . . my fever is a good deal abated this afternoon and the gout I am in hopes has left my head as it is much easier today but a gouty h[aze?] continues in my breast . . . it can hardly be said I have eat for the last 8 or 9 days.[74]

Almon concluded by signifying that he was too ill to continue writing. The early letters contain many such complaints.

A representative letter from Calcraft, who believed the country air might benefit Almon, invited his friend to visit him at Leeds Abbey:

> I am very sorry to read what you say about your Health. If Country Air is good for you, Come down here the latter End of the Week and have *that*, with Retirement in Perfection. Remember what I have suffered by neglecting myself, and let it be a Warning to You.[75]

Although Dr. Brocklesby was Almon's physician, on 5 August 1772 Calcraft, who professed himself to be greatly improved by one of Dr. Addington's treatments, urged Almon to consult Addington:

> Gout improperly treated has been the cause of my late sufferings—Do see Doctor Addington, He regards You, and will put You in a proper Way—On Monday he declar'd me safe, and order'd me to begin the Steel, Which I have done & it agrees.[76]

Shortly after offering this advice, Calcraft died.

Notes

[1] *The Indiana Quarterly for Bookmen*, IV (1948), 20–28.

[2] "Bookseller as Historian."

[3] Biography and letters, I, viii. To avoid confusion, at this point I should mention that, taken as a whole, this five-volume work is best described as a biography of Wilkes interspersed with letters in the manner of Mason's life of Gray or Boswell's life of Johnson.

[4] Almon's *History of the Late Minority* contains another treatment of these affairs, and, abbreviated though it may be, the version in his *Memoirs* still adds some new details, as does the account in *Biographical . . . Anecdotes*, II, 15–28.

[5] Biography and letters, I, 93–95. It may be recalled here that Wilkes, along with Churchill, founded the *North Briton*, with its antiministerial leanings, to counter Smollett's *The Briton*, a paper that supported Bute. Almon describes the origin of the *North Briton* in *Biographical . . . Anecdotes*, II, 9–12. For general background on the *North Briton*, see George Nobbe, *The North Briton: A Study in Political Propaganda* (New York: Columbia University Press, 1939). The curious circumstances of Almon's later connection with Smollett have been detailed by Lewis Knapp, *Tobias Smollett, Doctor of Men and Manners* (Princeton: Princeton University Press, 1949), pp. 280–82. Smollett's letter to Almon of 24 June 1770, which is first presented by Francesco Cordasco, ed., *Letters of*

Tobias George Smollett (Madrid: Imp. Avelino Ortega, 1950), pp. 35 and 44, should be regarded as a possible forgery. See Lewis Knapp, "Forged 'Smollett' Letters," *Notes and Queries*, 198 (1953), 163.

[6] For further details see George Rudé, *Wilkes and Liberty: A Social Study of 1763 to 1774* (Oxford: Clarendon Press, 1962), pp. 22–36.

[7] Presumably, the reason for using a general warrant here was the anonymity surrounding the publication of Number 45. Almon calculated that the same warrant used to arrest Wilkes was used to arrest some forty-eight people who were associated with the libel (Biography and letters, I, 99).

[8] *Ibid.*, I, 101. See also *Memoirs*, p. 15 and *Public Characters*, p. 125.

[9] Biography and letters, I, 102.

[10] See also *Memoirs*, pp. 15–16 and Biography and letters, I, 101–102. According to Almon, throughout, Wilkes was a surrogate for Temple because "as this was a matter in which his lordship could not publicly appear, it was agreed that Mr. Wilkes and the other injured parties should be the ostensible plantiffs in these causes (*Ibid.*, I, 132).

[11] "Bookseller as Historian," p. 78. There is some confusion about who exactly applied for the writ. See Audrey Williamson, *Wilkes: A Friend to Liberty* (New York: E.P. Dutton, 1974), p. 62. Although the writ was obtained, the Secretaries of State managed to evade it by shifting the custody of Wilkes, who was consequently committed to the Tower. In addition, as part of an attempt to secure evidence, Wilkes's house was ransacked and all of his papers seized. For this last act the indefatigable Wilkes later sued Halifax, Egremont, and Wood. After Wilkes was awarded damages, many of the others involved in the Number 45 affair instituted similar proceedings. See Raymond Postgate, *That Devil Wilkes* (New York: Vanguard Press, 1929), pp. 56–58; *Public Characters*, pp. 125–26; Rudé, *Wilkes and Liberty*, pp. 24, 28–29.

[12] See Brewer, p. 220, Postgate, pp. 53–63, Rudé, *Wilkes and Liberty*, pp. 24–29 and 193–94; Laurence Hanson, *Government and the Press, 1695–1763* (London: Oxford University Press, 1936), pp. 30–32, and P. Langford, *The First Rockingham Administration: 1765–1766* (London: Oxford University Press, 1973), p. 215.

[13] Here again, Almon gives the credit to Temple:

It is to EARL TEMPLE, and to him alone, that the nation owes the condemnation of general warrants, and the arbitrary seizure of persons and papers. Every body knows that Mr. Wilkes had not fortune sufficient to enter the lists with government. Earl Temple spared no expence; he relaxed in no exertion. Inflexible in his principles, firm in his resolution, he was the sinew of that authority which gave security to every man in his own house. In former cases of general warrants, the unfortunate persons had no protectors; and therefore they sunk under the weight of oppression: this was the first time that the arbitrary conduct of government in that respect was brought under a legal inquisition (Biography and letters, I, 135–36).

See also *Biographical . . . Anecdotes*, II, 27–28.

[14] Rudé, *Wilkes and Liberty*, p. 29.

[15] Biography and letters, I, 139. See also *Biographical . . . Anecdotes*, II, 29–30. Unless otherwise indicated, the details concerning the publication of *A Letter to Kidgell* in the following section are based on: *Public Characters*, p. 126; Rea, "John Almon: Bookseller to John Wilkes," p. 21; Postgate, pp. 65, 71–73; Rudé, *Wilkes and Liberty*, p. 30.

[16] This poem was privately printed by Wilkes in Westminster in 1763.

[17] Biography and letters, I, 18.

[18] *A Letter to J. Kidgell, Containing a Full Answer to his Narrative* (London: J. Williams, 1763), Almon's response to Kidgell's *A Narrative of the Poem*, ran through three editions (*Public Characters*, p. 127).

[19] *A Letter Concerning Libels* . . . was originally published as *An Enquiry into the Doctrine Lately Propagated, Concerning Libels, Warrants, and the Seizure of Papers* (London: Printed for J. Almon, 1764). The seven subsequent editions were entitled *A Letter Concerning Libels.* . . .

[20] Obituary, p. 1179; John Almon, *Biographical . . . Anecdotes*, I, 80. More recently, Smith attributed *A Letter Concerning Libels* to Temple (*Grenville Papers*, III, clvi-clviii), while Halkett and Laing attributed it to Dunning.

[21] For Mansfield's subsequent explanation of his order to change this text, see James Burrow, *Reports of Cases Argued and Adjudged in the Court of King's Bench* (London: Printed by A. Strahan and W. Woodfall for E. and R. Brooke, 1790), IV, 2532. For details of Almon's trial, see *Biographical, Literary, and Political Anecdotes*, I, 241–58; *Memoirs*, pp. 18–32; "A Short Retrospect of the Process against Mr. Almon, Publisher of the Letter on Libels," *Annual Register*, 8 (1765), 177–79; John Fox, "The King v. John Almon," *The Law Quarterly Review*, XXIV (1908), 184–98 and 266–78; John Fox, "The Summary Process to Punish Contempt," *The Law Quarterly Review*, XXV (1909), 238–54 and 354–71.

[22] When Almon's case first came to trial, the absences of the other justices forced Wilmot, who was reluctant to act alone in so important a matter, to postpone the proceedings. Almon's case was ultimately heard before Judges Wilmot, Yates, and Aston. The case for the prosecution was argued by the Attorney General, Sir Fletcher Norton (afterwards, Lord Grantley) and the Solicitor General, William De Grey (afterwards, Lord Walsingham). The case for the defense was argued by Sergeant Glynn and John Dunning (*Memoirs*, p. 23; "Short Retrospect," p. 177).

[23] For an understanding of this emphasis, it must be borne in mind that, as John Brewer has observed, Government and Opposition were generally in agreement over whether or not a given paper or pamphlet was a libel. What they argued about was procedure (Brewer, p. 220).

[24] In a trial by information (as opposed to indictment, whereby a grand jury presents the accusation), the prosecuting authority makes the charge based on information he has received from witnesses.

[25] "A Short Retrospect," p. 178. See also Fox, "The King v. John Almon," pp. 184–85, *Public Characters*, p. 121, and *Memoirs*, p. 25.

[26] The rule had been mistakenly entitled "The King against Wilkes" rather than "The King against Almon." See Almon's letter to Temple of 15 June 1765 in *The Grenville Papers*, III, 46–49; Fox, "The King v. Almon," p. 184; *Public Characters*, p. 130; *Memoirs*, pp. 27, 31–32; *Biographical, Literary, and Political Anecdotes*, I, 241–58. At one point during the trial when an attempt was made to issue a new rule, Almon was threatened with imprisonment and fled from London, even though his wife was pregnant. (The following day, Mrs. Almon went into labor.) See Almon's letter to Temple in *The Grenville Papers*, II, 65–68.

[27] *Memoirs*, p. 31. Although most sources follow Almon, according to Wilmot's son, proceedings against Almon were dismissed due to Norton's resignation as Attorney General. See John Wilmot, Esq., *Memoirs of the Life of the Right Honourable Sir John Eardley*

Wilmot [by his son] (1802; rpt. London: J. Nichols and Son, 1811), p. 76. See also John Campbell's *The Lives of the Chief Justices of England* (1845–57; rpt. New York: James Cockcroft, 1874), III, 190n.

[28] John Eardley Wilmot, *Notes of Opinions and Judgments Delivered in Different Courts by the Right Honourable Sir John Eardley Wilmot* (London: Hansard, 1802). See also Wilmot, *Memoirs*, pp. 76–80. In his two articles on Almon's trial cited above, John Fox shows that this procedure of punishing libels on the Court by summary process had no precedent before the eighteenth century. He argues that the right of the Court to punish libels on itself without a jury cannot be based on Wilmot's opinion in *Rex v. Almon* although this case has been frequently considered authoritative in modern decisions.

[29] Biography and letters, III, 140.

[30] *Ibid.*, III, 142.

[31] Add. MS. 30868 fo. 136.

[32] Add. MS. 30869 fo. 110.

[33] Add. MS. 30869 fo. 119.

[34] Add. MS. 30869 fo. 123. Wilkes also expressed his distrust of the post office in his letters to Almon (Biography and letters, III, 135, 138, 149, 168–69; *Memoirs*, pp. 30, 38, 41).

[35] Add. MS. 30868 fo. 136.

[36] Biography and letters, III, 140.

[37] Add. MS. 30869 fo. 123.

[38] Postgate, pp. 42–47; Nobbe, pp. 82–83. I have been unable to discover why Wilkes waited five years to print the letter.

[39] Temple, it appears, left much for Almon in matters concerning Wilkes. For example, after Wilkes's return to England and shortly before his first expulsion from Parliament, Almon, acting on Temple's instructions, advised Wilkes of Chatham's support:

> Last night my Lord Temple read to me a letter he had just received from Lady Chatham, assuring his Lordship *that Lord Chatham was strongly against the measure of expelling M' Wilkes*. These are her Ladyship's Words. My Lord Temple desired me to acquaint you of this acquisition to your cause, & he thinks that as soon as it is known it will check the foolish ardor of your malicious enemies. I had intended to have waited on you myself this morning, but had not opportunity. His Lordship desires, that in whatever may be thought proper to be said on this occasion, that his *name* may not be quoted (Add. MS. 30870 fo. 107).

[40] For details concerning the *Political Register*, see below.

[41] Add. MS. 30869 fo. 139.

[42] *Ibid.*, fo. 139. Almon again refers to the "foolish Letter about your duel with Ld Talbot" in Add. MS. 30869 fo. 157.

[43] Add. MS. 30868 fo. 136; Add MS. 30869 fos. 95, 110, 136, 139, 151, 153, and 157.

[44] Biography and letters of Wilkes, III, 133–47; *Memoirs*, pp. 35–44. Such references may be of use to scholars concerned with what Wilkes may have read when abroad.

[45] Add. MS. 30869 fo. 106. Almon often mentioned issues of the *Political Register* that he forwarded (Add. MS. 30869 fos. 123, 128, 153, and 157).

[46] On 30 October 1767 Almon wrote, "I keep no account of what I send: you are always heartily welcome to all my publications" (Add. MS. 30869 fo. 157).

[47] Add. MS. 30869 fo. 144. In the draft of a letter to an unidentified recipient, which, from its contents, was certainly written at a later date, Almon recalled this time:

> During the negotiation for a change of Ministers in the month of July 1767 the late lord Holland (Mr Foxs father) who held no place demanded an audience upon that occasion & was introduced into the Closet. The report at the time was that Lord H. advised the K [ing] to reject any arrangements which might be proposed to him that his M. [ajesty] might make any lord in waiting his minister. The power of the Crown was sufficient to support him. This fact was well known at the time it happened. It was told to me by M^r C Lloyd Mr Grenvilles private secretary by Mr Fitzhe[rbert] then member for Derbey by Mr Calcraft the present Lord Fortescue &c &c. (Add. MS. 20733 fo. 1).

[48] Add. MS. 30869 fo. 144.
[49] Biography and letters of Wilkes, III, 164–65.
[50] Add. MS. 30869 fo. 151.
[51] Add. MS. 30869 fo. 153.
[52] Brewer, p. 167.
[53] Add. MS. 30868 fo. 136.
[54] Add. MS. 30869 fo. 110. Coincidentally enough, around the same time Wilkes suggested that he, himself, edit a paper from Calais (Biography and letters, III, 138), an idea that Almon discouraged:

> As to coming to Calais & setting up a paper I think the project needless at least for the present; why should you put yourself to so much expence & trouble without a prospect of adequate advantage? If Paris is on any account improper or inconvenient Brussels in my humble opinion would suit you better (Add. MS. 30869 fo. 123).

In the same letter, Almon pointed to the liability of publishers:

> As to secrecy you may depend upon me in every thing you think proper to command. There is nothing you can print in France which I cannot as readily get done here. There is no difficulty in finding printers. The danger is in the Publication. He who disperses or distributes the copies is the Publisher & if the piece be of such a nature as to be particularly & enormously offensive & unguardedly written where is the use of printing it since it can be put into the hands of only a few?

[55] Add. MS. 30869 fo. 119.
[56] It should be noted that Almon's Political Register has no relationship to Cobbett's journal of the same name.
[57] Biography and letters, III, 142–43. See also Memoirs, p. 39.
[58] Add. MS. 30869 fo. 128.
[59] Add. MS. 30869 fo. 157.
[60] Brewer, p. 306.
[61] Biography and letters, III, 135, 138, 142–43, 147–49, 160, 164, 166–69; Memoirs, pp. 37, 39–43, and 45.
[62] Add. MS. 30869 fos. 123, 139, 153. Even so, Almon constantly solicited copy from Wilkes, ever reminding him of his promise of aid (Add. MS. 30868 fo. 106; Add. MS. 30869 fos. 119, 123, 128, 157).

[63] Add. MS. 30869 fo. 157. Although the *Political Register* ran to eleven volumes (or seventy numbers) from 1767 to 1772, Almon dissociated himself from it in 1768 because he feared the political consequences of publishing an account of "Lord B.'s visits" and of refusing to reveal his sources for a story on the Irish army (*Public Characters*, pp. 131–32).

[64] Inasmuch as Almon's part in Wilkes's *History of England* has been discussed at length by Robert Rea ("John Almon: Bookseller to John Wilkes"), here it is enough to note, with Lucyle Werkmeister, that Almon chose to mark the occasion of Wilkes's return by publishing this work: "Almon, who had always admired Wilkes, welcomed him back by bringing out . . . the introduction to his *History of England* . . ." (p. 111). The first volume of *The History of England from the Revolution to the Accession of the Brunswick Line*, which essentially consisted of the introduction, was the only part of the project that Wilkes completed. (It was printed for Almon in London, 1768.) The following year, Wilkes's cause was again championed in *A Letter to the Right Hon. George Grenville* (London: Printed for Isaac Fell, 1769), which is attributed to Almon by Watt and by Samuel Halkett and John Laing, *Dictionary of Anonymous and Pseudonymous English Literature* (Edinburgh: Oliver and Boyd, 1926). Almon, himself, however, assigned the *Letter* to Wilkes (Biography and letters, III, 300). This tract, which should not be confused with Almon's 1763 publication with the same title, took Temple's side in his dispute with Bute and with Temple's brother, George Grenville, who had supported Wilkes's arrest on a general warrant. Around this time Almon also published *Reflections on the Case of Mr. Wilkes* (1768) and *The Speech of a Right Honourable Gentleman on the Motion for Expelling Mr. Wilkes* (1769). For other works by and about Wilkes that were issued under Almon's imprint, consult appendix.

[65] Biography and letters, III, 171.

[66] Brewer, p. 167.

[67] Brewer, p. 167. *A Letter to his Grace the Duke of Grafton* (London: Printed for J. Almon, 1767), which is a truncated version of Wilkes's defense of his conduct and his criticism of Chatham's, contains new information about the general warrants brouhaha. Dated "Paris, 1766" and signed "John Wilkes," this tract went through eight English editions. In addition, it was printed in Paris and reprinted in Berlin.

[68] Add. MS. 30869 fo. 119.

[69] Add. MS. 30869 fo. 123.

[70] Biography and letters, III, 141–42; *Memoirs*, pp. 38–39. Similarly, on 25 May 1767, Wilkes wrote Almon, "I would not have you, a family man, run a risk for any party" (*Ibid.*, III, 143). See also Biography and letters, III, 166; *Memoirs*, p. 44. Robert Rea discusses *A Letter to . . . Grafton* in "John Almon: Bookseller to John Wilkes," pp. 23–25.

[71] Add. MS. 30869 fo. 106.

[72] Biography and letters of Wilkes, III, 136; *Memoirs*, p. 37.

[73] John Calcraft (1726–72), a wealthy politician, was M.P. for Calne from 1766 to 1768. Thereafter, from 1768 to 1772, he represented Rochester. (See below, chapter 4.)

[74] Perkins MS. XVIII-E (Papers in this collection have no folio numbers). Here it should be mentioned that, at the time, the term "gout" was used with much freedom. It was applied to a variety of symptoms that were otherwise undiagnosable.

[75] Perkins MS. XVIII-E (2 August 1772). See also *Memoirs*, pp. 85–86. Calcraft referred to his own illness in his letters of 30 May 1770, 21 November 1770, and 25 June 1772 (Perkins MS. XVIII-E). By 17 July 1772, Calcraft's health declined to the point that he described himself as "lost to the world from ill health" (Perkins MS. XVIII-E).

[76] Perkins MS. XVIII-E (*Memoirs*, p. 86). For medicinal purposes, steel filings were often taken internally. Another mode of treatment was to administer water that had been exposed to steel (OED). Samuel Johnson defined "steel" in its therapeutic sense as "chalybeate medicines." See *A Dictionary of the English Language* (1755; rpt. London: Printed for J.F. and C. Rivington, L. Davis, et al., 1785).

3
London Museum Trial and Fugitive Pieces

As should be evident, up until 1767 Almon's works and the works he published were, in the main, political. Yet Almon's emphasis was soon to change, as compiling literary collections increasingly became his main endeavor. Almon's collections, to be discussed below, are remarkable as the only "literary" work produced by a man devoted to politics. This is of far-reaching importance in evaluating the impact of political repression on Almon's career because, at the time he published his collections, legal problems made it difficult for him to publish or write politically sensitive material. Perhaps the reason for Almon's departure from his usual publications can help explain the nature of the departure itself.

In 1770 Almon was charged with libel for publishing one of Junius's letters. His trial raised significant general issues such as the extent to which a bookseller was responsible for the content of what he sold and how this, in turn, influenced the type of work he supported and the type of literature produced in the period. Indeed, Almon's politically inspired trial threw into relief the larger question of freedom of the press, the most powerful tool of the political opposition. These are the fundamental considerations that must be kept in mind when analyzing what occurred at this point.

On 19 December 1769 Junius's famous letter to the King (No. XXXV) appeared in Henry Sampson Woodfall's *Public Advertiser*. Here Junius criticized the policies and conduct of the King and went so far as to recommend that he be deposed. Expressive of the charged temper of the time, this forceful attack had an effect that can only be described as electric. By the next day, most other papers had reprinted it. Naturally enough, journals followed suit, and the letter soon appeared in nearly every newspaper and magazine in the nation. Yet the Attorney General, William De Grey, pressed libel charges against only six publishers. Besides Woodfall, proceedings were started against John Miller (for reprinting the letter in the *London Evening Post*), George Robinson (*Independent Chronicle*), Henry Baldwin (*St. James's Chronicle*), Charles Say (*Gazetteer*), and John Almon (*London Museum*). Out of these, only the cases against Woodfall, Miller, Baldwin, and Almon were actually brought to trial. And of all the publishers in England who had printed or reprinted the notorious letter, only Almon was convicted of libel.[1]

The others were tried in Guildhall in London before juries sympathetic to their cause. Lord Campbell, Mansfield's nineteenth-century biographer, emphasized the partiality of London juries in this instance:

> . . . no jury in the city of London would find a verdict against the publisher of JUNIUS, whatever they might be told from the bench as to their functions or duties (III, 382).

To be sure, in the case of Woodfall, the jury reached an ambiguous decision that was left unresolved. Miller and Baldwin were both acquitted.

In sharp contrast, the proceedings against Almon were conducted in Westminster, where juries generally cooperated with government. Indeed, as Almon's trial approached, Calcraft pointed to the jury as a potential problem. He expressed his concern in a letter dated 30 May 1770:

> I have been very ill, but am mending fast, and thankfull for Your Anxiety—I long to have Saturday well over, being truly sollicitous about Your Success—You have two good Council [Glynn and Davenport] & a good Cause, But I don't like the Middlesex Jurys—However there are bounds, People dare not stride over—If you want any

Assistance You know Where to find a Freind—Be sure. Let me hear
Saturday and Beleive me,

Faithfully Your's
JC[2]

Apart from the biased jury, several factors combined to operate against Almon, who was tried on 2 June 1770 in the Court of King's Bench before Lord Mansfield.[3] For libel trials, the power of the jury was limited to deciding whether the innuendo (in this case, the fact that "K---" represented "King") would be readily apparent to the average reader and whether the defendant actually published the work in question. The jury had no say in assessing whether it was libelous. Only the Court was empowered to determine whether the defendant was in fact guilty of libel.[4]

As outlined by the prosecution, then, the two potential sources of conflict centered around matters of innuendo and publication. Predictably enough, in his opening statement, De Grey charged Almon with these two infractions:

> The charge that is brought against the defendant with regard to this publication, contains two propositions: the one, that the publication concerns the king; his administration of government; of public affairs of the nation; the great officers employed in government; and the members of the House of Commons.—It likewise contains another proposition, *that the defendant published this writing.*—These are the two points, which it is necessary for those who support the information, to prove to your satisfaction, and that is all that is necessary for them to do.[5]

As for the innuendo, the critical question was the validity of the plaintiff's claim that most readers would immediately understand the letter as an attack on the King and his administration. Establishing this presented no particular problem—it was almost a foregone conclusion. Although at this point in the trial Sergeant Glynn, who represented Almon, attempted (unsuccessfully) to get his client off on a technicality, all sides agreed that the letter contained sufficiently clear innuendo. This fact, however, would obviously carry no weight if the

45

defense could prove that Almon had had no hand in its publication.[6] In short, Glynn was ultimately forced to base his case on the argument that his client did not publish the letter, despite the fact that his name appeared on the imprint of the *London Museum*.

Glynn attempted to defend this position on two grounds, both of which concerned Almon's intention. First of all, the counsel for the defense argued that the presence of Almon's name on the imprint in no way signified his involvement with publication. Glynn insisted that John Miller, the printer of the *London Museum*, had inserted his client's name without Almon's knowledge, let alone his approval. Miller confirmed this fact in an affidavit.[7]

Almon himself has told us of these arrangements, which he described as common practice:

> The printer of one of these monthly pamphlets, whose name was J. *Miller*, and resided near Pater-noster-row in the City, advertised his pamphlet (the London Museum he called it) to be sold *also* by J. *Almon* in Piccadilly. *Mr. Almon* gave him no authority for so doing, but it is pretty much the custom (since the metropolis has become so large and populous) for booksellers residing in one part of the town, to advertise their books, &c. to be had *also* of booksellers residing in *another* part of the town.[8]

In effect, this implies that the connections among publishers, printers, and booksellers were so entangled and overlapping that the presence of a name on an imprint may have been mainly a matter of exchange, distribution, and circulation. (Such possibilities, of course, potentially present bibliographers and other students of publishing history with major difficulties in dealing with the interpretation and general reliability of eighteenth-century imprints.)

The second feature of the defense argument concerned the sale of the libel. In this respect, the Crown's case against Almon was based on the principle that sale—which Almon maintained was his only offense, however indirect—was equivalent to publication. It seems to have been beyond dispute—and

Almon never denied—that the libel had been purchased in his shop. But Glynn held that his client was not liable as publisher of the letter because it had been supplied to him by Miller and sold in his shop by another party, all unbeknownst to Almon. More specifically, three hundred copies of the offending magazine had been sent to Almon when he was out of town. During this time, Almon's servant had sold sixty-seven copies, including several that, unfortunately, were bought by ministerial informers. When Almon returned and found the issue contained a libel, he halted its sale.[9]

Reasoning that, at least in this case, sale was not equivalent to publication, Glynn again focussed on the issue of intention, which, in many respects, was the most important aspect of his argument. Although Glynn urged that Almon was not responsible for the actions of his servant, Mansfield was unconvinced and declared:

> In the first place, as to the *publication*, there is nothing more certain, more clear, nor more established, than that the publication—a sale at a man's shop—and a sale *therein*, by his servant, is evidence, and not contradicted, and explained, is evidence to convict the *master of publication*; because whatever any man does by *another*, he does it *himself*. He is to take care of what he publishes; and, if what he publishes is *unlawful*, it is at his peril.[10]

The jury was instructed to disregard Almon's intention, to hold him responsible for his servant's actions, and to consider sale as tantamount to publication. After hearing unrefuted testimony that the magazine had been purchased at Almon's shop, the jury had no choice but to declare that the Junius letter contained an abundance of easily recognizable innuendo and that Almon published it. Unsurprisingly, Almon was found guilty of libel.

Reaction to the decision against Almon came quickly with such tracts as *Another Letter to Mr. Almon in Matter of Libel*.[11] Mansfield was attacked in a bitter letter from Junius and in both Houses of Parliament. In the House of Lords, Chatham and Camden condemned his conduct, while in the House of

Commons his decision was censured by John Glynn, John Dunning, and Edmund Burke. William De Grey, Edward Thurlow, and Charles Fox came to his defense.[12]

Better still, Almon's trial served as the occasion for reprinting the very letter that he was tried for "publishing." This time the letter appeared in *The Trial of John Almon . . . for Selling Junius's Letter to the K---*, which the *Gentleman's Magazine* accurately described as, in the main, "nothing more than a republication of Junius's letter, converted into an information by the Attorney General."[13]

The sole basis of the plea for a new trial again depended on the claim that the prosecution failed to prove that Almon had displayed criminal intentions. Although the defense advanced the argument that Almon could not be convicted of publishing a libel if he was ignorant of all facts concerning it, his request for a retrial was denied.

The larger ramifications of legally defining publication to include sale would make the bookseller responsible for the content of everything in his shop. (The point was not lost on Almon, who complained that it was "not in his power to read every book that is published.")[14] This would obviously have a bearing on the type of work that booksellers would be willing to support and sell and, consequently, on the literature of the period. Indeed, Almon's situation provides a particularly dramatic instance of the influence of law and politics on a bookseller and his output.

Almon was sentenced to pay a small fine and to put up eight hundred pounds security to insure his good behavior for two years.[15] With several exceptions, these legal restraints exerted pressures that governed the type of literature Almon published during this time. Here Almon's interpretation of his sentence is of primary importance:

> . . . this sentence, though calculated to appear light and moderate, is, in fact, most heavy, cruel and oppresive; as it amounts to a total

prohibition of [Almon's] following his trade or business as a book-seller. . . . without running the risque or incurring the forfeiture of the sum of eight hundred pounds; which would tend to [his] ruin.[16]

Almon most certainly realized that his sentence was meant to dictate the nature of his publications: ". . . *that* was the sole object; for if he [Almon] will print no more political pamphlets, he suffers nothing from the sentence."[17] Until the expiration of his sentence, Almon devoted himself primarily to his literary collection.[18] This clearly represents a divergence from his typical politically volatile publications.[19]

One way to determine the significance of Almon's collection is to compare it with Dodsley's *Collection of Poems by Several Hands,* commonly considered to have been the most popular collection of literature in the last half of the eighteenth century.[20]

Although no precise circulation figures are available, Almon's collection seems to have enjoyed considerable popularity. Whereas Dodsley's *Collection* expanded to six volumes and some thirteen editions were printed,[21] Almon's collection expanded to ten volumes; six editions of *The New Foundling* and eight editions of *An Asylum* were printed.[22] If commercial success can be considered an index of taste, the literature in Almon's obviously popular collection deserves some attention.

What, then, are we to make of these fugitive pieces? Although the dictionaries of Bailey (1730) and Johnson (1755) have entries for "fugitive," neither defined the word with regard to literature.[23] In one sense, however, Johnson defined "fugitive" as perishable and unstable. But only in the later dictionaries is the definition of "fugitive" as ephemeral applied to literature. For example, one definition is ". . . a fugitive piece; i.e. a little composition . . . which may be soon forgotten, or soon lost."[24] The date of the first OED citation of the literary application of "fugitive" is 1766 (Horace Walpole, however, used the term in this sense in 1758).[25] Nevertheless, the OED definition is instructive here: "Of a literary composition (occas. of a writer): Concerned or dealing with subjects of passing interest; ephemeral, occasional." Almon's collection illustrates these conceptions.

Perhaps the easiest way to approach the distinguishing features of Almon's fugitive pieces is to compare the content of Dodsley's and Almon's collections. James Sutherland expresses the typical view of Dodsley's poets and audience:

> We are safe in taking the reader of this miscellany as the typical poetry-reader of the period. . . . Dodsley's poets were men of culture writing for a reader who had enjoyed the same sort of education as their own, and who would therefore share their literary tastes and draw upon the same stock of knowledge. They assumed . . . that their readers would be tolerably familiar with at least the less recondite facts of ancient mythology.[26]

Dodsley's *Collection* was compiled to perpetuate and legitimize neoclassical standards. As the advertisement to this miscellany announced, its purpose was to

> . . . preserve to the Public those poetical performances, which seemed to merit . . . remembrance. . . . the Reader must not expect to be pleased with every particular poem . . . it will be sufficient, if nothing is set before him, but what has been approved by those of the most acknowledged taste
>
> (Advertisement, 1763 edn.).

Almon's collection, on the other hand, offers social commentary and was compiled to disseminate political ideas in a light-hearted manner and an economical format.[27] Almon wished to include

> . . . every article . . . that was thought worthy of Preservation . . . to render it as agreeable in the Pocket, as it is useful in the Library
>
> (Advertisement, 1786 edn. of
New Foundling).

The literature in Almon's collection is ephemeral and is more dependent on a knowledge of eighteenth-century society than of classical mythology.

As might be expected, Dodsley's *Collection* includes such eighteenth-century classics as Dyer's "Grongar Hill," Shenstone's "The School-Mistress," Green's "The Spleen," Collins' "Ode to Evening," and Johnson's "London" and "The Vanity of Human Wishes." Because of its ephemeral nature, however, the literature in Almon's collection, has, for the most part, become as obscure as Almon himself—despite the fact that it is by major eighteenth-century figures. For example, Almon's collection includes Wilkes's "The Thane of Bute," Walpole's "On Admiral Vernon," Churchill's "Extempore on Thomson's Willows," Chesterfield's "Epigram on Miss Eleanor Ambrose," and Garrick's "Advice to the Marquis of Rockingham."

Perhaps contrasting principles of selection for the two collections are most striking when they contain works by the same poets. For example, Dodsley includes Lyttelton's famous monody on the death of his first wife, whereas Almon includes one of Lyttelton's occasional pieces, his lines for a mask of children at Hagley. If Dodsley includes Gray's "Elegy" and "Ode on a Distant Prospect of Eton College," Almon includes his more political "Inscription for the Villa of a Decayed Statesman [Lord Holland]"[28] and "Jemmy Twitcher [Sandwich]." Other instances could be cited, but the point here is that while Dodsley preserved literature notable for its timelessness," Almon preserved literature notable for its timeliness.

Not only were the fugitive pieces in Almon's collection ephemeral in terms of their content, many were also ephemeral in terms of the context of their original publication. As the varying subtitles of Almon's collection announce, most of the compositions were previously published. Abstracted from the periodicals or newspapers where they first appeared, these pieces make little sense today. Consider, for example, Gray's ode on Grafton's installation. When this poem was published in the *London Chronicle* on 4 July 1769, it presumably presented few contextual problems for readers who would have remembered the description of the installation of the Duke of Grafton as Chancellor of Cambridge that had appeared several days earlier.[29] When the poem appeared in the *Gentleman's Magazine* for July, 1769, the same issue contained an account of the ceremony that mentioned the performance of Gray's ode composed for the occasion.[30] But when the poem came out in the *New Foundling Hospital for Wit*, it was unaccompanied by any such explanatory context.[31]

Similarly, when Garrick's "Advice to the Marquis of Rockingham" appeared in the *Annual Register* for 1765,[32] it would have undoubtedly been read as a celebration of the newly formed Rockingham ministry since the same volume of the *Annual Register* was filled with details concerning Rockingham's acceptance of the Treasury.[33] But when the poem appeared in the *New Foundling Hospital for Wit*, it was abstracted from its original context of publication, which would have made it easily understood.[34]

In sum, because of legal difficulties resulting from his activities as a bookseller, Almon, for the most part, stopped publishing and writing politically sensitive works and essentially turned to literary representation as an alternative outlet for political expression. Perhaps the reason for the comparative insignificance of both Almon's life and his collection in this century is that they are too firmly rooted in their time to allow the abstraction that would make them easily accessible to modern readers. What is now least accessible may, however, be what was most representative of eighteenth-century life and literature.

Notes

[1] Unless otherwise indicated, the following account is based on a combination of sources that includes: James Burrow, *Reports of Cases Adjudged in the Court of King's Bench* (Dublin: Caleb Jenkin, 1780), V, 2686–91; Campbell, III, 379–92; "Chronicle," *Annual Register*, 13 (1770), 115, 121, 165; "List of Books—with Remarks," *Gentleman's Magazine*, 41 (1771), 80–82; "Historical Chronicle," *Gentleman's Magazine*, 40 (1770), 541; *Memoirs*, pp. 61–76 (The text of the trial and of the motion for a new trial is appended to the *Memoirs*, pp. 167–236); Frederick Siebert, *Freedom of the Press in England*,

1476–1776: *The Rise and Decline of Government Controls* (Urbana: University of Illinois Press, 1952), pp. 385–88; David McCracken, *Junius and Philip Francis* (Boston: Twayne, 1979), pp. 91–93; *The Trial of John Almon . . . for Selling Junius's Letter to the K---* (London: Printed for J. Miller, 1770); Thomas Bayly Howell, *Complete Collection of State Trials* (London: Printed by T.C. Hansard for Longman, Hurst, Rees, Orme, and Brown, et al., 1814), XX, 803–867; *The Parliamentary History of England, from the Earliest Period to the Year 1803* [afterwards entitled *The Parliamentary Debates*] (London: Printed by T.C. Hansard for Longman, Hurst, Rees, Orme, and Brown, et al., 1813), XVI, 1211–1301 and 1312–22 (hereafter cited as Parl. Hist.).

[2] Perkins MS. XVIII-E. In his *Memoirs* Almon himself delineated the political leanings of the jury:

> . . . in striking the special jury, there was an obvious partiality; for although the King was party, several servants of the King's houshold [sic], and gentlemen in the public offices, were allowed to be of the forty-eight. Mr. *Almon* objected to several of these names, in the order they were mentioned, and said they were servants of his Majesty, who was party in the cause; but his objection was over-ruled . . . (p. 62).

Almon was forced to content himself with "leaving a clerk of the War-office for foreman, as a lesser evil than any of the twelve he was allowed to strike out" (pp. 62–63).

[3] Almon's description of Mansfield may be found in *Biographical . . . Anecdotes*, II, 209–366.

[4] These legal issues would not be resolved until the passage of Fox's Libel Bill in 1792.

[5] *Memoirs*, p. 168.

[6] It is significant, I think, that before he turned to the next aspect of his case (establishing that Almon was the publisher of the libel), De Grey attempted to anticipate and discredit arguments of the defense. In so doing, he contended that the publisher was at least as guilty as the author:

> What defense can be anticipated? . . . . If it is said, that the defendant is not the *author*? is then the *author* only to be punished? Is a man who *writes criminal*, and *he* who *disseminates* the *poison, innocent*? What signifies all the writers in the world, if they are confined to their garrets? and can't find publishers: they may write to eternity, and notwithstanding all their malignity they will do no damage. I am persuaded, that the man who introduces to the public the paper first written, is full as criminal as the writer (*Memoirs*, p. 172).

Of course, a necessary qualification in the present instance would seem to be that the identity of the author was unknown. In reply Glynn emphasized the difference between publisher and writer and argued for authorial responsibility.

[7] The same Miller, who had been charged with reprinting the libel in the *London Evening Post*, was never convicted. (See above.) Lucyle Werkmeister, who cites no evidence, for some reason assumes that Miller was Almon's "dupe" in this case (pp. 112–13).

[8] *Memoirs*, p. 62.

[9] The exact figures involved were revealed later in the motion for a new trial (Burrow's Reports, V, 2687).

[10] *Memoirs*, p. 182. After deliberating for two hours, the jury returned to obtain clarification of this point, whereupon Mansfield reaffirmed his position:

> I have always understood, and take it to be clearly settled, that evidence of a public sale, or public exposal to sale, in the shop, by the servant, or any body in the house or shop, is sufficient evidence to convict the master of the house or shop, though there was no privity or concurrence in him. . .
>
> *(Memoirs*, p. 185).

In the request for a retrial, Mansfield reiterated this stance, insisting that "the Buying the Pamphlet in the Public open Shop of a known professed Bookseller and Publisher of Pamphlets, of a Person acting in the Shop, *prima facie* is Evidence of a Publication *by* the Master himself" (Burrow's Reports, V, 2688).

[11] In his letter to Rockingham of 23 September 1770, Burke (no doubt correctly) attributes this pamphlet, which was printed for Almon in 1770, to Lord Camden. See Lucy Sutherland, ed., *The Correspondence of Edmund Burke* (Chicago: University of Chicago Press, 1960), II, 161. For Camden's opposition to Mansfield, see *Biographical . . . Anecdotes*, II, 367–402.

[12] Parl. Hist., XVI, 1211–1301. For Mansfield's explanation of his behavior, see Campbell, III, 387–90.

[13] "List of Books—with Remarks," p. 80. Interestingly enough, this tract was printed in London in 1770 for none other than John Miller.

[14] *Memoirs*, p. 71.

[15] On 21 November 1770, a day before Almon was to receive his sentence (delayed until 28 November), Calcraft wrote from Ingress to offer to stand bail for Almon:

> The Servant was Set off before I read Your Monday s letter. To day came the Other—If You want Bail to morrow I will be Counter Security to any body You will Get to attend The Court which my Health will not Permitt—If you want Money send some Freind down or an Express & Il Return a Draft by a careful Sev^t. Tho' I hope to be able to get up to The House tomorrow Where at this Time evry one should put the best Foot foremost tho' He Risques health—My attack has been in the Stomach & pretty Severe, but 'tis over I hope—Lord Temple has wrote me a most Affectionate Freindly letter wch pleases Me much, for many good Reasons—Write me all about The Remonstrance to Night—Poor Sawbridge is ill of a Fever. I write with Difficulty, But would not now neglect you (Perkins MS. XVIII-E).

Calcraft defended Almon in the House on 6 December (Parl. Hist., XVI, 1295–97). As he had reported in his reassuring letter of 2 September 1770, Calcraft previously enlisted Temple's aid on Almon's behalf (Perkins MS. XVIII-E).

[16] *Memoirs*, p. 71.

[17] *Memoirs*, pp. 74–75.

[18] Almon's collection consists of *The New Foundling Hospital for Wit*, which started as an annual periodical (*Memoirs*, p. 121), and *An Asylum for Fugitive Pieces*. Almon may have taken his idea from a previous catch-all collection of unusual poems and "curious pieces," *The Foundling Hospital for Wit* (London: Printed for G. Lion, 1743). See Arthur Case, *A Bibliography of English Poetical Miscellanies 1521–1750* (Oxford: Printed for the Bibliographical Society at the University Press, 1936 for 1929), pp. 319–22. Other literary works that Almon may have written during this time include *Letters Concerning*

the Present State of England (London: J. Almon, 1772), which contains an examination of theatre and of contemporary writers, and *Theatrical Biography* (London: Printed for S. Bladon, 1772), which deals with contemporary performers. See George Watson, ed., *The New Cambridge Bibliography of English Literature* (Cambridge: The University Press, 1971), II, 1802.

[19] It was once thought that Almon neither wrote nor published anything political during this period. [See, for example, *Public Characters,* pp. 132–33 and Bruce Gronbeck, "Almon, John," *Biographical Dictionary of Modern British Radicals* (1979), p. 18.] But the most recent information available, the on-line Almon file of the ESTC, indicates that several political pieces were, in fact, issued under Almon's imprint throughout this time. Although these seem to have been comparatively few, the ESTC is incomplete. Our understanding of Almon's publishing activities is therefore still subject to change.

[20] My evaluation of the popularity of Almon's collection depends on one major assumption: *The New Foundling Hospital for Wit: A Collection of Fugitive Pieces* and its continuation, *An Asylum for Fugitive Pieces,* were conceived of as a single collection. The advertisement for *An Asylum* makes this clear:

THE NEW FOUNDLING HOSPITAL FOR WIT being finished . . . this Volume entitled, AN ASYLUM FOR FUGITIVE PIECES, is humbly offered as a *Continuation of the Plan*; but under a different title, that it may not seem compulsatory on the purchasers of the former work to proceed. It is intended to publish a volume of this work occasionally, and to print it in the same size as the *New Foundling Hospital for Wit,* in order that such Gentlemen as chuse to have both, may bind them uniformly, whenever they please.

Although Almon published other compilations of fugitive pieces, he appears to have regarded them as discrete collections. These include: *Companion for a Leisure Hour: Being a Collection of Fugitive Pieces* (1769), *Fugitive Pieces of Irish Politics* (1772), and *The Fugitive Miscellany* (1774–75).

[21] Three editions of the first three volumes of Dodsley's *Collection* were published from 1748 to 1755, when the fourth volume came out. The complete *Collection,* including volumes one to six, was published ten times from 1758 to 1788.

[22] Six complete editions of the *New Foundling* were published from 1768 to 1796. Three editions of the first volume of *An Asylum* appeared from 1776 to 1785. A two-volume edition came out in 1779. The complete collection in four volumes was published four times between 1785 and 1799.

[23] In this connection, it should be noted that Johnson's introduction to the *Harleian Miscellany,* "An Essay on the Origin and Importance of Small Tracts and Fugitive Pieces" not only fails to consider fugitive pieces per se, but did not have this title in its first issue in 1744. See William Prideaux Courtney and David Nichol Smith, *A Bibliography of Samuel Johnson* (1915; rpt. Oxford: Clarendon Press, 1968), p. 15.

[24] *Johnson's and Walker's English Dictionaries, Combined,* 1828.

[25] There is some reason to believe that the "fugitive piece" became a widely recognized phenomenon in the second half of the century. This contention is borne out by the fact that no collections of fugitive pieces seem to have been published until around the middle of the eighteenth century, but from the middle to the end of the period, many such collections appeared. For example, Wing (1641–1700) lists no fugitive pieces. Similarly, Case lists no poetical collection with "fugitive" in the title or

subtitle. In passing it should be noted that although Foxon's primary interest is separately printed poems from 1701 to 1750, the word "fugitive" does not appear in the title of any of the poems that Foxon catalogued. Most convincing of all, a search through the computer-based ESTC files from 1700 to 1750 failed to locate any collection with "fugitive pieces" in the title or subtitle. The later part of the eighteenth century, however, witnessed the publication of many compilations of fugitive pieces besides Almon's. These include such collections as Horace Walpole's *Fugitive Pieces in Verse and Prose* [Strawberry Hill, 1758; see Allen Hazen, *A Bibliography of the Strawberry Hill Press* (New Haven: Yale University Press, 1942)]; *Fugitive Pieces* (London: Printed for T. Becket and P.A. De Hondt, 1767); Thomas Davies' *Miscellaneous and Fugitive Pieces* [London: T. Davies, 1773; see Courtney and Smith, pp. 116–17 and Katharine Balderston, ed., *Thraliana* (Oxford: Clarendon Press, 1942), I, 164]; Henry Headley's *Fugitive Pieces* (London: Printed for C. Dilly, 1785); *Fugitive Pieces: A Collection of Original Poems* (Edinburgh: Printed for J. Johnstone, 1797); and *Bell's Classical Arrangement of Fugitive Poetry* (London: Printed by J. Bell, 1789–97) in eighteen volumes. See N. Hardy Wallis, "*Fugitive Poetry*: An Eighteenth-Century Collection," *Essays by Divers Hands*, NS XVIII (1940), 43–66. Even Dodsley edited a work called *Fugitive Pieces* (1761), which Ralph Straus characterizes as "a rather weird collection"—see *Robert Dodsley, Poet, Publisher and Playwright* (New York: John Lane, 1910), p. 297.

[26] *A Preface to Eighteenth Century Poetry* (1948; rpt. Oxford: Clarendon Press, 1958), p. 54.

[27] *New Foundling Hospital*, III, 263.

[28] Gray's poem on Lord Holland was one of the few pieces that first appeared (without prior publication) in Almon's collection. According to R.W. Ketton-Cremer, Gray never intended to publish this satire. See *Thomas Gray: A Biography* (Cambridge: The University Press, 1955), pp. 228–29.

[29] "Ode to Music, Performed in the Senate House at Cambridge," *London Chronicle*, 26 (1769), 15–16; "The Ceremony Observed this Day at the Installation of the Duke of Grafton at Cambridge," *London Chronicle*, 26 (1769), 6–7.

[30] "Ode to Music, Performed in the Senate House at Cambidge [sic]," *Gentleman's Magazine*, 39 (1769), 359; "Historical Chronicle," *Gentleman's Magazine*, 39 (1769), 361.

[31] *New Foundling Hospital for Wit* (London: J. Almon, 1771), IV, 8–16.

[32] *Annual Register*, VIII (1765), 279.

[33] See, for example, *Annual Register*, VIII, 42–49; 166.

[34] *New Foundling*, II, 180–81.

4

Parliamentary Debates and Correspondence with Calcraft

Almon's collection of fugitive pieces shows that although Almon published few serious political efforts from 1770–1772 (the period covered by his sentence), he still retained a lively interest in politics. His role in reporting the debates in parliament and his correspondence with John Calcraft further demonstrate that Almon never fully relinquished his political activities during this time.

The significance of Almon's participation in the famous Printer's Case cannot be overestimated.[1] Although the House renewed its ban on publishing the proceedings of parliament on 26 February 1728 and made its resolution more comprehensive on 13 April 1738, monthly magazines continued printing the debates, often in transparently veiled form. But open defiance in the newspapers began only in 1768, when Almon started anonymously reporting the daily parliamentary debates (for the most part in undisguised fashion) in the *London Evening Post*.[2] Other papers followed suit. As George Rudé put it, "Led by John Almon . . . editors had begun to make it a regular practice to instruct and entertain their readers with detailed accounts of parliamentary proceedings."[3] Almon has described his initiative in the *Memoirs*:

> When the spirit of the nation was raised high by the massacre in St. George's-fields, the unjust decision upon the Middlesex election, &c.

Mr. *Almon* resolved to make the nation acquainted with the proceedings of Parliament: for this purpose, he employed himself sedulously, in obtaining from different gentlemen, by conversation at his own house, and sometimes at their houses, sufficient information to write a sketch of every day's debate, on the most important and interesting questions; which he printed three times a week regularly in the London Evening Post (p. 119).[4]

Although he began his reports in 1768, it was not until 1771 that Almon, in concert with Wilkes, was presented with the opportunity to press his view that parliament had no right to prevent the publication of its proceedings. According to D. Nichol Smith, "The crisis came in 1771, and the credit of forcing it belongs in the main to John Almon."[5] At this time parliament moved to take action against the printers of *The St. James's Chronicle, The Gazetteer, The General Evening Post, The Middlesex Journal, The Morning Chronicle, The London Packet, The Whitehall Evening Post,* and *The London Evening Post.*

The printers were ordered to attend the House, but Almon and Wilkes together persuaded Miller to disobey his summons. In Almon's *Memoirs* there is a convenient summary of the resulting clash between the City of London and the House:

A plan of resistance was settled by Mr. *Almon* and *Miller.* Mr. *Wilkes,* and some others of the city magistrates were consulted. When the messenger of the House of Commons came to take *Miller* into custody, a constable was ready; and the messenger was carried before the Lord Mayor, charged with an assault, as had been pre-concerted. Mr. *Wilkes* and Mr. *Oliver* were also at the Mansion-house. The assault was proved, and the messenger was admitted to bail. The Lord Mayor (Mr. *Crosby*) and Mr. *Oliver,* being members of parliament, were committed to the Tower; but Mr. *Wilkes* brought farther disgrace upon the House of Commons. They did not know what to do with him. At length they contrived an expedient as cowardly as it was contemptible. They made an order for him to attend on the 8th of April; and then adjourned to the 9th of April, to avoid their own order. During the debates upon this subject, which were very warm, several gentlemen, who were magistrates, declared they would act in the same manner in all such cases hereafter, and if any printers brought the messengers of the house before them, they would commit those messengers. Parliament now finding its own impotency in this business, abandoned the whole question entirely (p. 120).[6]

From this point on, parliament gave up further legal efforts, and printers exercised their right to publish the debates. A. Aspinall has pointed to the significance of the Printers' Case in terms of the growing public interest in politics:

> The year 1771 witnessed the famous struggle between the House of Commons and the printers of the London newspapers: a struggle which ended with the tacit abandonment by the House of its prescriptive but anachronistic right to prohibit parliamentary reporting. The ultimate result of this new freedom was to change the whole character of the constitution. The gradual creation of a politically educated public opinion was destined to make parliament, even in its unreformed state, increasingly sensitive to that opinion.[7]

In addition to his role in the Printers' Case, Almon filled a gap in the records of parliamentary proceedings by publishing a summary.[8] This covered the period from 1742, when Chandler's reports end,[9] until 1774, when Almon's own *Parliamentary Register* begins. Almon launched this journal to provide a monthly account of the debates and proceedings of both houses of parliament.[10] *Public Characters* recognized Almon's achievement in its description of *The Parliamentary Register*:

> This was the first production of the kind ever attempted. Hitherto the debates in parliament, very imperfectly given, and under Greek and Roman names, had been printed occasionally in some of the magazines. The work was very generally approved of, and several of the lords and members of the house of commons gave him considerable assistance (pp. 133–34).

Apart from Almon's contributions to the publication of parliamentary proceedings, he also maintained a more general interest in politics. Indeed, Almon's correspondence with John Calcraft is of considerable importance in any account of this period since both men were preoccupied with politics on local and national levels. The fragmentary evidence available in these letters, which include minute details about the English political scene, can often be verified by external sources and is almost always accurate.

Although Almon and Calcraft started corresponding in 1769, the greater part of the extant letters that passed between them date from 1771 to 1772, the year of Calcraft's death, and are located in the Perkins Library of Duke University.[11] This collection consists of some thirty-two signed autograph letters from Calcraft to Almon. Since these are reproduced in the *Memoirs*, they need only be quoted here when alterations show that Almon took considerable liberties in editing the text. In addition, among the Calcraft papers at Duke are eighteen autograph drafts of Almon's letters to Calcraft, which have never been published.

Before discussing the contents of the Almon-Calcraft correspondence, it seems appropriate to say something about Calcraft himself and about his relationship with Almon. John Calcraft (1726–1772) was a rich and powerful politician. (Contemporary rumor had it that his estates were worth in excess of ten thousand pounds a year.) Although Calcraft was early promoted by such friends as John Manners (Marquis of Granby) and Henry Fox (First Lord Holland), in 1763 he left Fox for Pitt, one of Fox's most formidable opponents. From 1766 to 1768 Calcraft held office as M.P. for Calne, and, by the time Almon and Calcraft started their regular correspondence, Calcraft was M.P. for Rochester, a position he held from 1768 until his death.

One way to examine the relationship between Almon and Calcraft is by using the manuscript version of Calcraft's letters as a check on Almon's editing techniques in the *Memoirs*. All editorial decisions that can without hesitation be assigned to Almon tend to go in one direction: He consistently expunged lines that show evidence of the real dynamics of their friendship. Thus, the true nature of this relationship may be located in Almon's deletions.

In an effort to present himself not as Calcraft's factotum, but, rather, as his friend, Almon edited out of the *Memoirs* references to his bookselling activities undertaken on Calcraft's behalf. (Although it could be argued that this information is omitted because it is trivial, Almon retained many insignificant details in the *Memoirs*.) Consider, for example, Calcraft's letter of 7 January 1772. In the edited version, which may be found on page 83 of the *Memoirs*, Almon left out Calcraft's entire order: "Do send me a hundred of your best Pens or the best you can get for my own writing with 11 Quires of . . . Fools Cap—a Bible . . . for A Girl of 8 Years old . . . ."[12]

Almon consistently deleted lines such as these, presumably in an attempt to hide the financial basis of his political friendships. For instance, when Calcraft was preparing to travel to Italy for health reasons, he again engaged Almon's services. In the *Memoirs*, Almon published news of the trip:

> I continue to recover daily, but am advised not to risk the next winter in England, so shall set out in about two months for Italy. But shall hope to see you more than once in that time (p. 84).

Then follows the portion of the original letter that Almon deleted:

> A Strong Box for carrying Papers . . . I shall want, and wish you to look about and see whether any good one is to be had ready made. If not . . . [w]e may in time think of Contriving one. . . . You will know the proper Maker, better than I can tell you, and no time should be lost as I find by Experience, great Disappointments arise from the Uncertainty of People keep[ing] to their Promises in these trifling Undertakings.[13]

From the *Memoirs* Almon also dropped Calcraft's further orders concerning this subject:

> Before Mr Almon orders the Strong Box, Mr Calcraft desires to know upon what Plan he intends to have it made, & to hear fully of his Design.
> Pray order my News Papers to be directed to Leeds Abbey near Maidstone by Tuesday's Post, and so continue till further Order.[14]

All this is omitted from the *Memoirs*, thus leaving us with a very different impression of the relationship between Almon and Calcraft.

There were other changes. For instance, by clever editing techniques, Almon altered a notice intended for insertion in the newspapers so that it would appear to be a letter to himself from Calcraft. According to the *Memoirs*, Calcraft's letter read:

> Yesterday came on the election of a Mayor for the City of Rochester, for the year ensuing, when Mr. Alderman *Hulkes* was chosen with the hearty consent of his fellow-citizens; notwithstanding every attempt was used to damp their spirit, and bias their choice in favour of Alderman *Sparkes*, who belongs to the Chest at Chatham, and is an active instrument of administration. This point was carried with great spirit, in spite of every attempt of government, who found they could not succeed, and at last gave up the point. *Hulkes* is above temptation, like yourself; a steady friend to the public, and to me (p. 79).

The manuscript version presents a different impression:

> Yesterday came on The Election of a Mayor for the City of Rochester for the Year ensuing when Mr. Alderman Hulkes was chosen with the hearty consent of His Fellow Citizens notwithstanding evry attempt was us'd to damp their Spirit & Bias their choice in favour of Mr. Ald^m Sparkes who belongs to the chest at Chatham and is an active Instrument of Administration—
> Do insert the above or somewhat to the same purport. The Point is with great Spirit in spite of evry attempt of Goverm^t Who found they could not succeed & at last gave up the Point. Hulkes is above Temptation. And Like Yourself a steady Freind to the Publick, as well as to me.[15]

If Almon received Calcraft's announcement too late to place it for him, the obsequious tone of his reply to Calcraft leaves no doubt of Almon's subservient position:

> I sincerely congratulate you upon your late success at Rochester but am very sorry I was not home when your letter came otherwise the article it contained should without fail have appeared immediately. If all other persons of weight & interest were equally in [Earnest?] the

Public would not complain of the Neglect of the Great nor the ministry so often have cause to triumph. You must see with pleasure from this instance that wherever the people are countenanced they fail not to make a warm return. I beg leave to return you many Thanks for your venison Your exceeding goodness I do not deserve though my best endeavors shall not be wanting.[16]

As this incident suggests, Calcraft often used Almon to gain access to the press. For example, on 13 January 1772, Calcraft instructed Almon:

If you put in paragraphs, put that Mr. [Philip] *Francis* is appointed Deputy Secretary at War, and continues his present employment also. It will teaze the worthy secretary, as I well know, and oblige me. I will give you my reasons, when you will find more folly in that noble Lord, than even you thought him capable of. This may be an interesting week. Pray continue your attention to your country friend.[17]

Apparently responding to Almon's reply, which, unfortunately, does not appear to have survived, Calcraft defended this ploy:

I was not misinformed; I knew *Francis* was not Deputy, but wished him to be so; and to cram the newspapers with paragraphs that he was so. For he is very deserving (*Memoirs*, p. 84, n.d.).

From every indication, it seems clear that Calcraft not only employed Almon to fill his book-selling orders, but manipulated him to insure that Almon would publish the material he provided in the various newspapers with which he was connected. While it is true that Calcraft never hesitated to use Almon, their connection was all the more remarkable because, as far as we know, they remained on friendly terms. (It seems, however, by no means unlikely that such an arrangement was typical of many comparable relationships between wealthy politicians and political booksellers.) Although Almon and Calcraft wrote little that is especially revealing from a personal standpoint,[18] two or three extracts from their correspondence show that Almon and Calcraft met (or, at the very least, expressed a desire to meet) frequently. For instance, in one of Almon's drafts he regretted missing a visit from Calcraft: "I am very sorry I was not at home when you obligingly called."[19] Of a similar nature was Calcraft's letter of 15 October 1771, where he invited Almon to Ingress.[20] Again, on 25 October 1771, after inviting Almon to visit him, Calcraft added, "My only business is to make any spare days you have for the country, comfortable to you, because I have a real confidence in, and friendship for you."[21] In succeeding letters Calcraft often mentioned his desire to see Almon. On 11 November 1771 Calcraft wrote: "On Saturday I go to Dorsetshire; will try to see you as I pass town,"[22] and several days later, he once more proposed to visit Almon in London.[23]

The correspondence between Almon and Calcraft is of great general interest insofar as it concerns the (often interrelated) politics of London and of the nation. As should become apparent, their letters substantiate the impression that, more often than not, both men had the benefit of "inside information." (In some measure they had Wilkes and Temple as common points of reference.)

In September, 1771 Almon and Calcraft were engrossed by the election for Lord Mayor of London. As early as 20 September, Almon described his recent conversation about the mayoral race with Wilkes, who supported the re-election of Brass Crosby, and, to this end, promoted the return by the Common Hall of Crosby and William Bridgen for final selection by the Court of Aldermen:

> Mr. Wilkes called upon me this Evening. I can perceive he is somewhat disconcerted by the common Hall & that he has no plan nor is there any plan framed by his friends expecting the Election of LordMayor. Indeed he says that though alderman Bridgen has declined—yet the Livery will return him. . . .[24]

Almon went on to report his attempt to effect a reconciliation between Wilkes and John Sawbridge, who, along with Robert

Bernard, Richard Oliver, and John Horne, had broken with Wilkes:

> I proposed to Mr. Wilkes an Idea to return alderman Sawbridge with the present Lord Mayor [Crosby]. To which he coldly said he had no objection. But I doubt his sincerity as the proposal was not his own. I know him too well not to be convinced that his vanity and [distance?] are unconquerable. . . . If Mr. Sawbridge was to come forwad & give some proof or promise of a total separation from Mr. Horne he might recover himself. . . . But the dispute will be between Crosby and Nash. . . .[25]

On 26 September 1771, Almon was concerned with advancing Crosby's candidacy:

> The approaching city Election is at present the [only?] subject of Conversation. . . . I have and will do all I can to get Crosby returned. . . . Alderman Bridgen . . . in decline has had such an effect upon the minds of the citizens that Mr. Wilkes' friends have been obliged to give up the idea of that nomination.[26]

After predicting much backing for Sawbridge and Crosby, his own favorites, Almon correctly anticipated the Court's endorsement of William Nash: "Mr. Nash's friends are to meet today to consider what they shall do. . . . The Court will certainly support Nash and [whatever?] friend with him. . . ."

In his letter of 2 October 1771, Calcraft emphasized his agreement with Almon and took notice of the dispute between Sawbridge and Horne: "Sawbridge was duped by Horne, contrary to all resolutions formed before he saw him. Altogether it is not to be thought of with patience."[27]

On the same day Almon accurately forecasted the outcome of the election:

> This days poll I think has decided the Election The return will be Nash and Sawbridge & Nash will be chosen by the aldermen. Though the Court may think they shall be able to return Halifax instead of Sawbridge but that is impossible. . . .[28]

65

As Almon had foreseen, the Common Hall (in part because opposition leaders were at odds) returned Nash and Sawbridge to the Court of Aldermen, which, in turn, elected Nash.

From the letters of Almon and Calcraft quoted above, it would appear that the two were absorbed with London politics. But, throughout this time, their interest in national politics was equally important. With regard to the country as a whole, both men numbered among their friends (or had some contact, however limited, with) most of the prominent political figures in eighteenth-century England. Their letters are filled with what seems to be first-hand knowledge of the political strategies of men such as John Wilkes, Edmund Burke, and Lords Shelburne, Temple, Rockingham, North, and Chatham. They also commented on Henry Luttrell, Junius (and Philip Francis, often considered as a likely candidate for Junius), Lord Mansfield, and David Garrick. Indeed, Almon's informed pronouncements would have been next to impossible without strong personal connections.

As one might expect, some of Almon's most interesting drafts concern Lord Temple. The first of these letters is dated 10 November 1771 and details a recent conversation with Temple about political tactics. Since it refers to the continuing goodwill between Temple and Chatham, it is reasonable to suppose that this letter was of special interest to Calcraft, who had served as their mediator several years earlier:

> Lord Temple came to town yesterday in very good health. I saw his lordship this morning. His conduct will be mostly the same this winter as last. I took the liberty to say you were in town on Thursday and asked very affectionately after him. He did the same of you. Lord Chatham & his lordship are quite well together. He says it would be [unwise?] to take a part now when every thing has been lost by the folly of others. By lying aloof he may come forward with more force on any crisis. . . . He thinks too that by leaving the ministry to themselves they will soon quarrel and destroy each other. . . .[29]

For his part, Calcraft made frequent inquiries about Temple

and found in Almon a willing source of information. For example, on 13 January 1772 Calcraft asked:

> Pray tell me, in confidence, what did Lord *Temple's* visits to St. James's mean? Does he talk as loudly in commendation of Lord *North*, as the ministers and their friends boast, at Lady *Primrose's* particularly, as well as other places (*Memoirs*, p. 83).

By way of response, Almon stoutly denied this rumor:

> Your suspicions about L[ord] T[emple] are without foundation. But he comes tomorrow night. I shall see him next morning. Be assured you shall be informed exactly.[30]

Almon seems to have known (and recorded) minute details about Temple's activities and feelings. For instance, there is one draft still extant in which Almon, apparently after conferring with Temple, described his reaction to the forthcoming wedding of Thomas Lyttelton (son of Temple's first cousin George). We have Almon's word for it that Temple was pleased with the prospect of Lyttelton's marriage to Apphia Peach, the widow of Joseph Peach, who had been Governor of Calcutta. In the same letter Almon speculated about the reasons for another impending marriage—that of Lord Hardwicke's daughter to Lord Polwarth (later Baron Hume):

> Lord Temple is in perfect health at Stowe. He is exceedingly rejoiced at the approaching marriage of Lord Lyttelton's with a Mrs. Peach (a widow lady, possessed of a large fortune acquired in Asia) which affords Lord Lyttelton the greatest happiness as well as giving much pleasure to all the friends of his family. The Youth may perhaps be reformed & the money is convenient. . . . Lord Marchmont has contrived a match between his son . . . & Lord Hardwicke s eldest daughter. . . . Thus, you see the cunning of the Scot to get an English Peerage into his Family.
> Lord Rockingham mends but slowly[31]

There is reason to suppose that Almon was also in close enough contact with both Rockingham and Shelburne factions to allow him to delineate their activities. For example, on 15 January 1772, Almon described the interplay between the two camps:

> There is a whisper today that the Rockinghams intend to be active. I doubt it but shall know in a day or 2. If they are active it is probable the Shelburnes will not, & vice versa.[32]

The following day Almon predicted that Shelburne would become entangled in a situation of assumed political importance, the threat that Henry Luttrell would vacate his seat in the House. Behind this potential crisis there were a number of problems concerning Wilkes:

> I thank you exceedingly for the Brawn it is the best I ever eat. . . . I . . . hear (by way of report only) the Rockinghams mean to be inactive. Col. Luttrell I believe will do something but he will not communicate with any person. He will not say what he intends to do. Yet he says (for so Govr Pownall told me this morning & [he is] good authority, because they are much together) that he has been misrepresented as to abusing the ministry he does not abuse them he does not even speak of them because it would detract from his merit. . . . These were his words from which it is clear he means to do something. With regard to the Shelburne's the probable thing is they will try to take advantage of whatever steps Luttrell may take & if he should desire to vacate his seat they will affirm Wilkes is incapable of being elected on account of his being sheriff.[33]

Related to these potential changes was another, perhaps more significant, possibility. Almon wrongly surmised that, under the impact of these events, the North ministry would be dissolved:

> . . . the K[ing] finding Lord N[orth] has not been able or capable to keep him out of this scrape will dismiss him & take in the Shelburne's. It is true all this is but conjecture but it has the appearance of being probable.[34]

The remaining issues in the correspondence between Almon and Calcraft may be briefly described: In June of 1772, Almon and Calcraft were concerned with the bankruptcy of Alexander Fordyce, the great Scottish banker.[35] In addition, they considered the stock market,[36] as well as the Royal Marriages Act[37] and the possibility of Lord Hillsborough's resignation from his post as colonial secretary.[38] Although a tremendous amount of what Almon reported was undoubtedly based on gossip, rumor, and innuendo, he seems to have been privy to information about everything from the East India Company[39] and the Irish cotton laws[40] to the Spanish intrusions in the West Indies.[41]

Examination of Almon's activities at this stage in his career has indicated that, comparatively speaking, Almon himself published few political works until the expiration of his sentence. Instead, he channelled his political efforts into parliamentary reporting. In addition, Almon's letters to Calcraft demonstrate that his interest in politics continued unabated. All these factors must be borne in mind when considering what occurred next.

Notes

[1] Unless otherwise indicated, the following account is based on Almon's *Memoirs*, pp. 118–121; Almon's Biography and letters of Wilkes, V, 51–63; Haig, pp. 102–118; D. Nichol Smith, "The Newspaper" in *Johnson's England: An Account of the Life and Manners of his Age*, ed. A.S. Turberville (1933; rpt. Oxford: Clarendon Press, 1952), II, 353–56; Peter D.G. Thomas, "John Wilkes and the Freedom of the Press (1771)," *Bulletin of the Institute of Historical Research*, XXXIII (1960), 86–98; Peter D.G. Thomas, "The Beginning of Parliamentary Reporting in Newspapers, 1768–1774," *The English Historical Review*, LXXIV (1959), 623–36; Rudé, *Wilkes and Liberty*, pp. 155–65; *Biographical . . . Anecdotes*, I, 403–408.

[2] The precise nature of Almon's involvement with this paper is unclear. In his *Memoirs* (p. 119) Almon identifies John Miller as the printer, and in his Biography and letters of Wilkes (V, 52n), Almon claims to have been an owner. Yet, advertisement duties levied against Miller during these years indicate that he was the registered publisher/proprietor. See A. Aspinall, "Statistical Accounts of the London Newspapers in the Eighteenth Century," *The English Historical Review*, 63 (1948), 226.

[3] *Wilkes and Liberty*, p. 156.

[4] We have no surviving copies of *The London Evening Post* for 1768 and 1769; however, Peter D.G. Thomas has convincingly confirmed Almon's statement in "The Beginning

of Parliamentary Reporting in Newspapers, 1768–1774," pp. 625–31, where he concludes that in 1768 Almon was the "foremost reporter" of the debates in parliament (p. 628) and until around 1774, "Almon remained the leading reporter" (p. 631).

[5] "The Newspaper" in *Johnson's England*, II, 355.

[6] In his biography of Wilkes, Almon described the inception of their plan: ". . . it was immediately concerted between Mr. Wilkes and Mr. Almon, that if the printer of the London Evening Post should be complained of, a serious, a bold, and a strong resistance should be made" (V, 57–58).

[7] "The Reporting and Publishing of the House of Commons' Debates 1771–1834" in *Essays Presented to Sir Lewis Namier*, ed. Richard Pares and A.J.P. Taylor (London: Macmillan, 1956), p. 227.

[8] *The Debates and Proceedings of the British House of Commons . . . Compiled from Authentic Papers*, 11 vols. (London: Printed for J. Almon and S. Bladon, 1766–75).

[9] Richard Chandler, ed., *The History and Proceedings of the House of Commons from the Restoration to the Present Time* (London: Printed for Richard Chandler, 1742–44).

[10] Although this project continued until 1813, Almon was associated with it only until 1780, when John Debrett took over the venture.

[11] Perkins MS. XVIII-E.

[12] Perkins MS. XVIII-E.

[13] Perkins MS. XVIII-E (3 July 1772).

[14] Perkins MS. XVIII-E (5 July 1772). In another letter dated July, 1772, Calcraft asked Almon to perform still another task (Perkins MS. XVIII-E).

[15] Perkins MS. XVIII-E (17 September 1771).

[16] Perkins MS. XVIII-E (20 September 1771).

[17] *Memoirs*, p. 83. I have been unable to locate a newspaper version of Calcraft's notice.

[18] As previously noted, however, they did exchange complaints about their health. (See chapter two above.)

[19] Perkins MS. XVIII-E (n.d.).

[20] *Memoirs*, p. 81.

[21] Perkins MS. XVIII-E; *Memoirs*, p. 81.

[22] Perkins MS. XVIII-E; *Memoirs*, p. 81.

[23] Perkins MS. XVIII-E; (14 November 1771).

[24] Perkins MS. XVIII-E. For further details on the mayoral election of 1771, see Ian Christie, *Wilkes, Wyvill, and Reform: The Parliamentary Reform Movement in British Politics 1760–1785* (London: Macmillan, 1962), pp. 45–57; George Rudé, *Hanoverian London 1714–1808* (Los Angeles: University of California Press, 1971), pp. 169–70; Rudé, *Wilkes and Liberty*, pp. 165–68. The Court of Aldermen had the right to choose the Lord Mayor from two candidates nominated by the Court of Common Hall, which was composed of members of the City's livery companies. For information on the government of London, see Sidney and Beatrice Webb, *English Local Government from the Revolution to the Municipal Corporations Act* (New York: Longmans, Green, and Co., 1906).

[25] Almon was partially mistaken—the Common Hall eventually returned, not Crosby and Nash, but rather Sawbridge and Nash.

[26] Perkins MS. XVIII-E.

[27] Perkins MS. XVIII-E; *Memoirs*, p. 80.

[28] Perkins MS. XVIII-E.

[29] Perkins MS. XVIII-E.

[30] Perkins MS. XVIII-E (15 January 1772).

[31] Perkins MS. XVIII-E. Although this draft is undated, to judge from its contents, it was probably written in 1771 or 1772: Lyttelton returned from a trip to Italy near the end of 1771 and was married on 26 June 1772. Almon's interview with Temple must have taken place during this interval.

[32] Perkins MS. XVIII-E.

[33] Perkins MS. XVIII-E (16 January 1772). Earlier Almon had reflected on the possibility that Luttrell's resolution was backed by the ministry "who think they shall get rid of Mr. *Wilkes* by his being Sheriff. (*You may be assured Mr. Wilkes will not permit an election. He will say there is no vacancy, and go to the House and demand his seat.*)" In the same place Almon had taken up the matter of Shelburne's position:

> Either Col *Luttrell* has not formed his plan, or he has a point to carry with the ministry. Opposition mean to lie by, and wait for new events. Mr. *Dowdeswell* said this last Friday to several gentlemen. Lord *Shelburne* has said, within these few days, that though he shall always be happy to act with, and submit to Lord *Chatham*; yet if Lord *Chatham* finds it convenient to retire, he shall think himself at liberty to pursue his own line. There is much meaning in this. The *Shelburnes* are negotiating, or holding themselves out for negotiation. They are first oars at Buckingham-house. Lord Temple is very well. I was at Hayes yesterday (12 January 1772; *Memoirs*, pp. 82–83).

[34] Perkins MS. XVIII-E (16 January 1772). Luttrell's threat came to nothing; North did not leave office until 1782.

[35] *Memoirs*, p. 84; Perkins MS. XVIII-E (n.d.).

[36] *Memoirs*, pp. 79–80.

[37] Perkins MS. XVIII-E (22 February 1772).

[38] *Memoirs*, p. 85; Perkins MS. XVIII-E (17 July 1772 and 2 August 1772). Around the same time, Will Burke had informed Charles O'Hara of Almon's intelligence: "My friend Almon tells me for certain that Lord Hillsborough is going out. . . ." See Ross Hoffman, ed., *Edmund Burke, New York Agent with his Letters to the New York Assembly and Intimate Correspondence with Charles O'Hara 1761–1776* (Philadelphia: The American Philosophical Society, 1956), p. 530. Matters came to a head several weeks later, when Hillsborough left office. (He was succeeded on 14 August 1772 by the Earl of Dartmouth.)

[39] Perkins MS. XVIII-E (26 September 1771).

[40] Perkins MS. XVIII-E (28 December 1771).

[41] Perkins MS. XVIII-E (4 November 1771).

5

Political Publications, the American Revolution, and Retirement

Although Almon, with certain exceptions, refrained from publishing political material while his sentence was in effect, his interests, as we have seen, still exhibited an underlying consistency. Predictably, after this interval there was a radical change in the nature of his publications. The shift in Almon's publishing ventures can best be understood if we consider his transactions with William Mason and his professional activities during the American Revolution, an event that brought Almon into the orbits of Benjamin Franklin and Edmund Burke, prompted his pro-American publications, and filled his correspondence with details regarding the situation in America.

When Almon resumed publication of politically sensitive works, one of the first pieces he supported was *An Heroic Epistle to Sir William Chambers* (1773), an anonymous response to Chambers' *Dissertation upon Oriental Gardening,* which had been issued in the spring of 1772. Ostensibly an attack on the famous architect, this satire was actually more concerned with politics than with horticulture. It was directed against such targets as Sir Fletcher Norton (for accepting valuable sinecures), the Rev. John Horne (for deserting Wilkes), Lord Bute (for his Tory politics), Lord Mansfield (for his methods of meting out justice), and even the King himself (for his notions of personal rule).

So curious are the details attending the publication of the *Epistle* that it seems worth examining this project in some detail. Almon apparently never discovered that the poem had been written by William Mason (possibly with the assistance of Horace Walpole).[1] A close examination of the correspondence between Walpole and Mason, who devote a good deal of space to Almon, reveals much dissimulation, secrecy, and intrigue on the part of both participants.[2]

For example, Mason intentionally and rather gleefully fostered confusion over the attribution of the *Heroic Epistle*. In his letter to Walpole of 7 May 1773, Mason, with a characteristic sense of self-importance, related a recent conversation with Lord Holdernesse. Here Mason went so far as to compare himself to Junius:

> Our talk was entirely on general subjects and literary matters, such as
> . . . the *Heroic Epistle*; I controverted none of his opinions, only, as he
> seemed to think that the *Epistle* had merit, I ventured to say that I
> thought it worthy of Soame Jennyns had it suited his political senti-
> ments. He replied, "So it was, but S.J. would never have used that
> *harsh* kind of satire." From his Lordship's account I find that it is
> generally supposed to be Temple Lutterell's, although Almon declares
> it to be the work of a young man and his first work. After all, we live
> in an age of miracles that two such writers as he and Junius should keep
> themselves concealed.[3]

Almon's interest in the *Heroic Epistle* was, of course, far from purely political. There were also motives of a strictly commercial nature.[4] As the preface to the poem makes clear, Almon cleverly promoted it by his timing:

> This poem was written last summer [the summer of 1772] after the
> Publication of Sir William Chambers's *Dissertation*; but the bookseller,
> to whom it was offered [Almon], declined publishing it, till the town
> was full.—His reason for this is obvious.

John Draper rightly assumes that Almon's intentional delay in publishing this satire was indeed warranted, for "the 'town' consumed a dozen editions in as many months" (p. 84).

Judging by the number of editions, the *Heroic Epistle* evidently enjoyed immense popularity. According to Draper, "Everyone read it: before the end of the year, eleven editions had come out; and by 1777, a fourteenth was found necessary" (p. 250).[5] Mason and Walpole also deceived Almon about Mason's authorship of (as well as Walpole's connection with) the *Heroic Postscript*, which Almon was to publish in 1774. In his letter to Mason of 14 January 1774, Walpole voiced his fear of being associated with the *Postscript*, which satirized George III and praised the press. He urged Mason, if necessary, to "manage" Almon, whom he accused of being "a rogue":

> Dr _____ delivered it [the *Postscript*] to me with great marks of apprehension, and protested he knew not what it contained; that he was ordered to deliver it to a person who was to call for it: this struck me extremely; the person I conclude is Almon, whom I know and have found to be a rogue. He has already bragged, such a poem was coming out, and remember if he guesses the author, that you must manage him. Money will be offered him to tell, and he will take it and tell. Hence arises my first difficulty, and on your account, who I am sure would not for the world hurt Dr _____ whom Almon will name.[6] My next difficulty is relating to myself. . . . [W]hat could I say, if the Doctor should name me? I never could tell a lie without colouring, and I trust you know that my heart is set on acting uprightly; that I lament my faults, and study to correct myself. . . . Do not imagine that a man who thinks and tells you he should colour if he lied, would betray you to save his life. I give you my honour that I have not, to the dearest friend I have, named you for author of the other, nor would for this. I can answer for myself; I cannot for the Doctor. . . . The result, therefore, of all is that I wish you could contrive to convey the poem to Almon without the intervention of Dr _____, whom I may mistake, but who seemed uneasy; and as he did not venture to trust me with his knowledge of the contents, I am not in the wrong to be unwilling to trust. I will keep it till I get your answer; and shall enjoy reading it over and over. If it is more serious than the former, though it has infinite humour too, the majesty of the bard, equal to that of the Welsh bards, more than compensates. If it appears, as I hope, I will write to you upon it, as a new poem, *in which I am much disappointed, and think it very unequal to the first*. . . . It will be hard if my letter is not opened at the post, when we wish it should.[7]

From Mason's reply of 15 January 1774, it appears that Walpole's reaction was excessive and unfounded: "You are under much greater apprehensions than you need to be on this subject. . . . The person who was to call for it was not by any means him whom you suspect [Almon]."[8] After informing Walpole that he was employing an intermediary, as in his last negotiations with Almon, Mason went on to reassure him about his association with the *Heroic Postscript*:

> If after all you have any fears as being made privy to it, I give you full liberty to burn it instantly, and as there is no other copy extant you may be assured it will perish completely. A[lmon] knows nothing about the matter yet, and was it now in his hands would make no use of it till the beginning of a new month for his own pecuniary reasons.[9]

Such, then, is the history of Almon's relationship with William Mason. In the meantime, Almon was becoming increasingly interested in the dispute with America. Almon's publishing activities in connection with Benjamin Franklin, whom he compared to Czar Peter the First as "the projector and founder of his country's greatness and power,"[10] may be mentioned as an example of Almon's early efforts on behalf of the American cause. In the summer of 1767, Almon published the first English edition of *The Examination of Doctor Benjamin Franklin, Relative to the Repeal of the American Stamp Act*, an account of Franklin's testimony of 13 February 1766 before the House of Commons (Committee of the Whole).[11]

In 1774 Franklin was instrumental in persuading Almon to publish *An Appeal to the Justice and Interests of the People of Great Britain in the Present Dispute with America*, which is now generally attributed to Arthur Lee.[12] With the hope of enlisting Almon's aid, Franklin enclosed the manuscript of this pamphlet, which argued that England had no right to tax the colonies, in his letter to Almon of 7 November 1774.[13] Almon's response, dated 6 December 1774, reveals his commercial attitude towards the venture:

There having been only a small number printed, because upon so beaten a subject, one is doubtful of success, till the Public opinion can be taken; but this pamphlet being much approved, it is probable that it will be reprinted. Should be glad therefore of notice of any errors (per penny post, or otherwise). . . .[14]

Since the *Appeal* did, in fact, prove to be popular, Almon ultimately published four editions. (It was subsequently reprinted in New York.)

There seems to be no question that Franklin regarded Almon as pro-American in his sympathies. Franklin encouraged fellow colonists to send American tracts to Almon to be reprinted in England.[15] In addition, Franklin, along with William Bollan and Arthur Lee, authenticated Almon's version of the petition to the Crown from the Continental Congress over a rival edition published by Thomas Becket.[16]

The petition was also of interest to Edmund Burke, whom Almon would supply with intelligence on more than one occasion.[17] Burke's first letter to Almon that has survived is dated 6 August 1775. As Almon explained in his *Memoirs* (pp. 93–94), where the letter first appears, it deals with the anticipated arrival of Richard Penn, Jr., with the petition from the Continental Congress to the King. Almon had apparently given Burke, who expressed his gratitude for the information, advance notice of this impending diplomatic visit:

> I am obliged to you for your early communication of the intelligence you have; and wish most ardently that this opening towards a reconciliation on the part of America may be improved by the ministry here and prove the means of a lasting peace to this empire.[18]

Several months after this letter, Burke referred to the letters of Valens, which appeared in the *London Evening Post* from 1775–76.[19] In 1777 Almon collected and published these pieces, which discussed affairs in Ireland and America and condemned the war.[20] Almon later attributed them to Richard Burke (brother of Edmund) with the assistance of William and Edmund.[21] It is possible that Almon took the hint for his collected edition from Ralph Izard, the wealthy American Revolutionary from South Carolina. On 4 August 1776 Izard had suggested that Almon compile these letters:

> I am so well pleased with the productions of Valens . . . that I think you should reprint them all. They are no longer the property of the Author, & the public have a right to [receive?] them at your hands. Several Editions of Junius appeared before the Authors with a Preface Dedication, & Appendix. Valens may follow the example of Junius.[22]

It is not until 3 February 1779 that we find what appears to be the next letter in the known correspondence between Almon and Burke. Here Burke was evidently replying to a letter from Almon which, unfortunately, seems not to have survived. The letter under consideration relates to a request from Almon to publish a verbatim account of Admiral Keppel's trial:

> It would, I assure you, give me great pleasure to serve you in any manner in my power, with regard to the business upon which you have written to me: and if I had been at Portsmouth when your letter arrived, I should have given it an immediate answer. I find that the Admiral leaves the publication of the Trial, with all the emoluments which arise from it, entirely to the short-hand writer; and does not interfere with him in any part of the disposition. If this had not been his plan, I am very sure he would give you the preference. I am very sensible of your zeal and good wishes, in a cause which naturally interests every man, who has any concern for the public.
> I am, with great regard,
>   Sir, your most obedient and humble servant,
> EDM. BURKE.
> The Admiral just tells me, that he is very sorry he is engaged; for that if you had applied before his leaving town, you certainly should have had it (*Memoirs*, p. 111).[23]

A record of Keppel's court-martial was subsequently published "by the desire of a society of gentlemen" (who are not identified on the imprint) on 13 February 1779.[24] But Burke was eventually able to intercede of behalf of his friend, and the following month Almon published another version of the trial.[25]

78

Burke is found writing his next recorded letter to Almon on 26 December 1779.[26] According to John Woods, this note refers to *Substance of the Speeches Made in the House of Commons, on Wednesday,the 15th of December, 1779. On Mr. Burke's Giving Notice of his Intention to Bring in a Bill after the Christmas Recess, for the Retrenchment of Public Expences, and for the Better Securing the Independence of Parliament.*[27] Burke's tract, published by Almon in 1779, summarized his first speech on economic reform.[28] Burke instructed Almon on how to handle the publication:

> I thank you very much for the active attention with which you have supplied the loss which happened by the accident of Friday Night. You will look over the correction yourself and circulate the paper according to directions sending a dozen Copies hither. I am ever with Very great regard and the compliments of the Season.[29]

This letter closes Almon's known correspondence with Burke. From the foregoing account of Almon's activities, it would appear that he was often engaged in publishing British works related to America and in printing and reprinting American political pieces.[30] As Almon reflected in his *Memoirs*, "American writers constantly sent him their pamphlets and papers to be re-printed in England" (p. 33). In addition, Almon seems to have exchanged much information with American printers.[31]

One reason Almon was everywhere expected to be an authority on the crisis with the colonies was that from 1775 to 1784 he published *The Remembrancer*, which proved to be an unqualified success (Sabin 955).[32] Although Almon was sympathetic to the American cause, his stated intention was to use his appropriately entitled journal to preserve ephemeral documents related to the American Revolution:

> The late interesting advices from America suggested the utility of a periodical collection of the best accounts of every important public transaction. Several events are expected during the summer, which probably will be the subject of discussion next winter. Many of these accounts being published in the newspapers, are frequently mislaid after the day of publication, and when afterwards wanted, are some-

times very difficult to recover: besides, being mixed with the common occurrences of the day, and published in the large folio size, render that mode of preservation awkward, disagreeable, and almost impossible.[33]

Of course, as publisher of *The Remembrancer*, Almon had access to privileged information from many channels.[34] It seems to have been generally known that Almon had both a means to disseminate information and a number of important American contacts who provided him with a wealth of knowledge about American affairs. In his *Memoirs* Almon recounted an anecdote which, while it is no doubt an exaggeration, suggests that he was regarded as an expert on the situation in America:

> A few months previous to the commencement of hostilities, the Duke of Grafton was called upon in the House of Lords (the secretary of state not being present) to inform the House, what number of the king's troops were in America? which he answered: he next was asked, what force the Americans had? To this question the Duke replied, that he did not know; but that those who wanted such information, might probably obtain it by applying to Mr. *Almon* (p. 93).

Indeed, many did just that. Among the Almon papers in the British Library are numerous letters thanking Almon and/or asking him for information about affairs with America.[35] For example, consider Almon's letter from Ralph Izard of 16 October 1777 from Paris, where Izard was acting as an American diplomatic representative:

> I left London without giving you such a direction as would conduct your Letters to my hands unopened. I should be very glad to receive your communications as often as possible, & the fuller they are, the more acceptable they will be to me. Frequent, & authentic information on the state of affairs will be of greater importance to me than I was aware of when I left England; it will not only be a gratification to me, but may put it in my power to be of service to the cause, which if I am not much mistaken in you, you have very much at heart, as well as myself. . . . The greatest part of the news that we ever have here, is brought from England. Dispatches from the Congress do not arrive very frequently. Some of the Vessels which are charged with them fall

into the hands of the enemy, others when chased frequently too hastily throw them overboard. Two which come under the latter description have very lately arrived safe in France. The last authentic accounts from Congress are of the beginning of August. Without descending to particulars it will be satisfactory for you to know that every thing had a most promising appearance, and there was nothing like dismay to be seen in any part of the Continent. With regard to France, the ministry here are determined if possible to avoid a war, at the same time they continue to afford very substantial assistance to those who are in want of it, which assistance, I doubt not, will be effectual. . . . I send this to you by a private hand, who has promised to deliver it safely to you. I beg that you will on no account let anybody know that I have written to you, as there are good reasons for secrecy. It is not likely that I shall be able to give you much information from hence. Let me know however how I can safely address you by the Post. The last Remembrancer that I have is N° 4; continue to send them regularly if possible. . . .[36]

Like Izard, many of Almon's correspondents provided him with information. Foremost among these was John Lloyd, whose letters can convey some sense of the extent of Almon's knowledge. The first letter of their known correspondence was written by Lloyd from Bristol on 21 September 1775, after news of the Battle of Bunker Hill had been received in England. Here Lloyd reported on the condition of the regiments of Thomas Gage, Royal Governor of Massachusetts, whose troops had suffered heavy losses in that engagement:

> Having on my journey down made an excursion into Bucks and Oxfordshire, I did not get here before yesterday, when I had the pleasure to receive your favours of the 15th and 16th inst. and for which I am particularly obliged, as also for your kind intention to continue your communication of interesting intelligence. . . .
> Yesterday a Ship arrived here which left Boston the 21st Aug. She has brought upwards of forty passengers, who confirm the deplorable state of Gage's Army, and further say it was the general opinion, that the provincials were meditating some grand and important undertaking: this is all the material intelligence that I have obtained, if anything more transpires from them deserving your attention, it shall be transmitted. . . .[37]

Lloyd's next letter to Almon is dated 29 September 1775 from Bristol. Again Lloyd began by thanking Almon for providing him with information. The most noteworthy feature of this letter is that it contains an extract of a letter Lloyd had received from an unidentified source in Charleston, South Carolina. The extract is in Lloyd's hand and is dated 5 August 1775. In an unmistakeable tone, it stressed the determination of the colonies to resist the British:

> Be assured, Peace will never be [word unintelligible] established between Great Britain and America, until the latter receives an ample recognition of her rights, and a full satisfaction for the blood that has or may be shed. The inhabitants of this vast continent would give up all their Sea Coast towns [move?] in to the interior Country, and contentedly subsist on the bare necessaries of Life, rather than submit to the implicit subjugation of a British Parliament. But don't apprehend they will suffer this distress like docile animals. No, depend they will protect their property, to the last extremity, and altho they have hitherto acted only on the defensive, believe me, unless there was evident prospect of accomodation this winter, hostilities will commence . . . by and with the assistance of a foreign power. . . . And then farewell to Great Britain.[38]

Lloyd's letter of 30 July 1776 finds him at Southampton.[39] For an understanding of the context of this letter, it should be remembered that the colonists had been defeated at Quebec near the end of 1775. By May of 1776, most of the Patriot army had withdrawn from the area. The following month John Burgoyne was sent to Canada to reinforce Sir Guy Carleton. Together they managed to occupy Crown Point:

> I am thankful for your intelligence: the satisfaction I received from it was in some measure counter balanced, by the news from Canada; the provincials most certainly do not conduct their affairs in that Country with the necessary spirit and resolution, and unless there is a very material alteration in their management of the War, in that quarter, they will soon be in a very precarious situation.[40]

In the same letter Lloyd sent further word of the war efforts:

Amongst the many who have resorted to this place there are some who appear to be well informed respecting political matters and from whom I learn that there is no unison in the Cabinet . . . that the French and Spanish Courts gave very evasive answers to some questions lately asked by the British ambassadors, respecting their naval equipments, and that in consequence it was resolved in Council to fit out a fleet of the line; The number and [word unintelligible] of the Ships I have no doubt but you are well informed of—You may depend upon it as a fact, that the Ministry have advises wch mention the capture of two or more transports with Six hundred & seventy soldiers (I suppose them to be Highlanders). . . .

The supreme lethargy which arises from the general spirit of dissipation, that manifestly pervades the whole kingdom, will prevent the people seeing their danger, till they are brought to the very brink of destruction.

If you have published a remembrancer since I left town . . . direct it for me at Mr. Penford's.

At about the same time, in his letter to Almon of 22 August 1776,[41] Lloyd addressed the question of American support for the Declaration of Independence, which had, of course, been approved by the second Continental Congress:

I am informed from good authority, that the Declaration for Independence was not carried unanimously in Congress, and that the dissentient voices were consequential: If so, I think a door may be open for the exercise of that trite maxim in politics, "Divide et impera" and upon which, I really believe, administration have still their greatest dependence for success in their infernal plan of subjugation.[42]

Lloyd went on to express his confusion over recent events in America:

I suppose by the time you receive this letter, it will be no news for you to hear, that the Ranger Sloop is arrived at Portsmouth. . . . [A] gentleman of this town brought the intelligence from thence yester-evening. The particulars of her dispatches were kept secret, except the loss of the Actaeon frigate on Charleston bar, which information leads me to apprehend there has been an expedition against the town, and yet I cannot reconcile the supposition to the well known orders to Clinton to join Howe.

Lloyd was, in fact, correct on both counts: Although Henry Clinton and Peter Parker had unsuccessfully attacked Charleston, South Carolina in June, 1776, by August Clinton had arrived at Staten Island to reinforce William Howe.

In his next letter to Almon, dated 9 October 1776 from Southampton, Lloyd solicited information about the situation in New York. Here it should be remembered that the fighting on Long Island had begun in the middle of August, when Howe forced Washington to retreat to Brooklyn. Further British victories drove Washington out of Brooklyn, and, by 15 September, the British had captured New York. Battles in the area continued and, shortly after the present letter, Howe drove the colonial army out of White Plains:

> I beg leave to renew my request, that when your leisure permits, you will be pleased to favour me with your intelligence. . . .
>
> Pray what do you think of the report from France of an action on Long Island? It is certainly an event to be expected. I have seen letters from Officers at Staten Island, which mention in the most express terms, that preparations were making for an attack, and that many days would not elapse before it would be made.
>
> The infamous system of Colonial government has lost America. I have no doubt but her Independency will be effectually established. It is not in the power of this country to make America an adequate compensation for the injuries she has sustained; therefore no reconciliation can be expected.[43]

Almon's next known letter from Lloyd, dated 17 October 1776, provides a remarkable account of one of the German mercenaries serving in Howe's forces on Long Island:

> I have been favoured with reading an Officer's Journal from Long Island, and there from have selected the following anecdote, which may perhaps be new to you.
>
> In Pensylvania are settled a vast number of Germans among the troops from that State, there was taken on Long Island a Captain who happened to be a native of Hesse. Having fallen into the hands of a Hessian officer, he carried him to the General Heister who expostulated with the Captain on the impropriety of his own, and his Countrymens behaviour towards Great Britain, and in particular to his Majesty King

George. The Captain, in a spirited tone of voice, replied, that he had no King, nor would he acknowledge one: upon which the General knock'd him down, and when he had recovered, ordered his Servant to bring two glasses of wine, when he compeled the Captain to take one and on his bare knees to drink the King's health, and then dismissed him.[44]

Lloyd's last extant letter to Almon (dated 22 December 1776 from Southampton) need not be transcribed here, as it simply contains further questions about the fighting in New York and the likelihood of foreign intervention.[45]

John Sykes, Almon's former teacher (above, chapter one), also figures as one of Almon's most informative correspondents. Sykes's letters, many of which are of some historical interest, consist largely of details related to Liverpool from 1778–80. As his letter of 11 March 1778 indicates, Sykes's chief preoccupation during these years was recruiting a regiment:

> The inclosed hand-bills are distributing by our worthy mayor, soliciting a subscription towards raising a new regiment. They are doing the same at Manchester. I wish I was able to say any thing in favour of affairs at Liverpool. . . . I believe Liverpool feels the effects of the American war, more severely than any town in England (*Memoirs*, p. 104).

In the same month Sykes provided specific statistics concerning progress in the recruitment campaigns at both Liverpool and Manchester:

> Our recruiting goes on very well, we have got upwards of 600, besides those we have no Acct. of from the Country. A week ago I got an authentick Acct. from Manchester, when they had 823.[46]

In his letter to Almon of 22 October 1778, Sykes detailed his recent conversation with Sir William Meredith, who represented Liverpool in parliament from 1761–80.[47] Through Sykes, Meredith relayed information to Almon about the change in Liverpool's attitude towards the War:

> Sir W. Meredith is at present here, yesterday he sent for me to dine with him & almost the first word he spoke to me was to ask when I heard from my old Friend Almon? What you said, &c. &c. He desired me to tell you that he finds people's sentiments here very different from what they were 12 months ago, with regard to the American war. . . .

Presumably this reaction set in when news of the French treaty of alliance with the colonies, negotiated in February, 1778, reached Liverpool. Sykes also described a further, related concern, increasing ship-building activity:

> As to our trade, we are at present all Life—fitting out privateers with the greatest avidity. This may perhaps likewise turn out to be one of our Follies; but the great success our adventurers have met with since Commissions were granted against the French, induces every one to hope for the same success—I was much obliged to you for a sight of Mr. Kennion's Letter. . . .[48]

I have tried to convey some sense of Almon's political interests by quoting extensively from manuscripts of letters, many of which are not readily available. Other letters could, of course, be cited, but by now the extent of Almon's involvement in the American Revolution should be apparent. In the meantime, an event of some importance was happening in Almon's personal life.

Almon's poor health (above, chapter two) may have prompted him to purchase some country property in Hertfordshire in 1775,[49] but his wife's illness was probably the most compelling reason for their move from London in June of 1781. At this time John Debrett, who at one point had been Almon's partner, bought his business.[50] Almon's early retirement was generally considered to be an indication of his wealth.[51] According to his obituary in the *Gentleman's Magazine* (p. 1179):

> Mr. Almon . . . by a sedulous application to business, and a fortuitous chain of events, became possessed of a very handsome fortune, and at one time aspired to a seat in parliament. On better consideration,

however, he concluded it would be more prudent to retire from business; which he did, with a decent competence, to a pleasant villa at Boxmoor. . . .

But Almon could hardly have enjoyed his prosperity, as he became increasingly alarmed by the declining health of his wife. The extent to which this affected Almon should not go unnoticed. We learn about Almon's life during this difficult period partly from his poetry, and partly from his vast correspondence. Naturally enough, Almon's mind was filled with personal preoccupations. Of his retirement to Hertfordshire and the condition of his wife, Almon wrote:

> I built a house: to steal from time
> A few more years, and cheer the ray
> Of life's cold evening, ere the prime
> Of sweet enjoyment felt decay. . . .
> The heart was good, the head was wrong;
> I meant to eke the date of life;
> To pass the social hours among
> My friends, my children, and my wife.[52]

According to Almon, he tried desperately to heal his wife, whose fate was "suspended," as it "stood betwixt/Returning health, and weak'ning pain."[53]

Apart from Almon's poetry, letters from his friends confirm both his attachment to his wife and his assiduous care of her during her illness. For instance, Dr. Brocklesby took particular notice of Almon's efforts on her behalf when he emphasized that Almon had "left nothing untried, that art, friendship, and every kind office . . . could procure for her."[54]

Yet, despite Almon's constant attention, on 31 August 1781, Elizabeth Jackson Almon died:

> With eager haste I clasp'd my arms
> Around her snowy neck:
> She strove to speak, but death alarms;
> She from th'embrace must break.

Then parting from me clos'd her eyes,
    I seal'd 'em with a kiss;
Each limb extended lifeless lies,
    —Those limbs of former bliss.[55]

A further mark of Almon's regard for his wife is his profound sense of remorse at her death. Describing himself as a "disconsolate husband," Almon had the following inscribed on her tombstone in Bovingdon Churchyard in Hertfordshire:

For thee my thoughts all pleasures shall forego,[56]
For thee my tears shall stream in silent woe.
First taught by thee the highest bliss to prove,
The force, the truth, the purity of love;
Sacred to thee the gift I will confine,
Join thee at death—and be for ever thine.[57]

A year later, Almon would still lament her death as the occasion when he found "ev'ry pleasure fled!"[58]

Worried about what he termed Almon's "melancholy condition," Dr. Brocklesby invited him to London, hoping that this would help "alleviate . . . too anxious concern for one who is irrecoverable."[59] It was not, however, until several years later that Almon would move back to the city. And it is to the years after Almon's temporary retirement that I now turn.

Notes

[1] "Monthly Catalogue," *Monthly Review*, NS XLVIII (1805), 105; John Draper, *William Mason* (New York: New York University Press, 1924), pp. 250–51; W.S. Lewis, Grover Cronin, Jr., and Charles Bennett, ed., *Horace Walpole's Correspondence* (New Haven: Yale University Press, 1955), XXVIII, 81; Allen Hazen, *A Bibliography of Horace Walpole* (New Haven: Yale University Press, 1948), p. 152. William Mason (1724–97), a poet and clergyman, is now perhaps best known as the friend, biographer, and editor of Thomas Gray, who dubbed him "Scroddles." As Leslie Stephen put it, "Mason was a man of considerable abilities and cultivated taste, who naturally mistook himself for a poet" (DNB). Mason's friendship with Horace Walpole began after Gray's death, when he requested information from Walpole for his edition of the life and letters of their mutual friend. After the publication of Mason's work in 1775, his correspondence with Walpole continued until the early 1780s, when they had a falling-out, and their correspondence all but ceased.

[2] Even so, it was probably Walpole who recommended that Almon publish Mason's poem. See Walpole's letter to Mason of 2 June 1782 in W. S. Lewis, Grover Cronin, Jr.,

and Charles Bennett, ed., *Horace Walpole's Correspondence* (New Haven: Yale University Press, 1955), XXIX, 253. Almon had earlier published Walpole's defense of General Conway, *A Counter-Address to the Public on the Late Dismission of a General Officer* (London, 1764). See *Biographical . . . Anecdotes*, I, 64–65.

[3] Lewis, Cronin, and Bennett, ed., XXVIII, 82.

[4] It was previously mentioned that Almon received all the profit from most of the works he published since they were prepaid. Even so, Almon did finance a certain number of publications, including the work under discussion. From Mason's letter to Walpole of 7 May 1773 and Walpole's reply dated 15 May 1773, it appears that Almon paid ten pounds for the satire (Lewis, Cronin, and Bennett, ed., XXVIII, 81–82 and 88).

[5] The correspondence between Walpole and Mason also points to Almon's unorthodox methods of advertising his publications. In his own time, Almon seems to have been regarded as a shrewd—if something less than honest—businessman. For example, in his letter to Walpole of 17 June 1775, Mason complained of being attacked for omitting Gray's poem on Lord Holland's villa from his edition of Gray. Mason guessed that "Philo-Gray," his critic in the papers, was none other than John Almon. Almon, he reasoned, was using this ploy to advertise his *New Foundling Hospital,* where the poem first appeared:

> A man who styles himself Philo-Gray of Salisbury has twitted me in the newspaper for not publishing a complete edition of Gray, because I have omitted the stanzas on a decayed statesman. . . . I suspect it is Almon in order to sell his own *Foundling Hospital for Wit* where those verses are printed (Lewis, Cronin, and Bennett, ed., XXVIII, 209).

The Yale editors of Walpole have been unable to locate the newspaper article.

[6] Robert Rea defends Almon against Walpole's distortions and exaggerations. In addition, he exonerates Almon from Walpole's charges that he accepted bribes in the course of publishing several of Mason's satirical poems. See "Mason, Walpole, and that Rogue Almon," *Huntington Library Quarterly,* XXIII (1960), 187–93.

[7] Lewis, Cronin, and Bennett, ed., XXVIII, 126. The identity of the doctor remains unknown.

[8] Lewis, Cronin, and Bennett, ed., XXVIII, 128–29. In passing it should be noted that in his letter to Walpole of 3 March 1774, Mason begrudgingly commented on Almon's large profit from the *Heroic Postscript,* which ran through at least eight editions (XXVIII, 137).

[9] Almon was soon to publish other works by Mason, who continued to "Bind in poetic sheaves the plenteous crop,/ And stack [his] full-ear'd load in ALMON's shop" (*Heroic Postscript*). In 1776 Almon published Mason's "Ode to Mr. Pinchbeck upon his Newly Invented Patent Candle-Snuffers, by Malcolm Macgregor, Author of the *Heroic Epistle*. . . ." The following year Almon published his *Epistle to Dr. Shebbeare: to which is added an ode to Sir Fletcher Norton. . . .* (Almon's successor, John Debrett, published Mason's *The Dean and the 'Squire* in 1782.) In addition, Mason was well represented in Almon's collections, where Almon printed or reprinted many of his pieces: Almon's *Asylum for Fugitive Pieces in Prose and Verse* (1785 edn.) included "Ode in Commemoration of the Glorious Revolution, 1688" (III, 196). *The New Foundling Hospital for Wit* (1786 edn.) contained Mason's "Heroic Epistle to Sir William Chambers" (II, 5),

"Heroic Postscript" (II, 17), "Ode to Mr. Pinchbeck" (II, 23), "Epistle to Dr. Shebbeare" (II, 30), "Ode to Sir Fletcher Norton" (II, 43), "Dean and 'Squire" (II, 52), "In Memory of Mrs. Mason" (VI, 44), and "Epitaph on Miss Drummond" (VI, 44).

[10] *Biographical . . . Anecdotes*, II, 176–77. (Almon's sketch of Franklin appears on pp. 175–344.)

[11] *The Gentleman's Magazine*, 37 (1767), 368–72, was quick to print extracts of Almon's edition of *The Examination*, which had previously been published in Philadelphia by Hall and Sellers in 1766. Extracts also appeared in the *London Chronicle*, 22 (1767), 21, 25–26. One of Almon's correspondents Hugh Williamson, a physician from Philadelphia, discussed *The Examination* in his letter to Almon of 11 December 1766 (Add. MS. 30733 fo. 145; *Memoirs*, p. 33).

[12] Lewis W. Potts, *Arthur Lee: A Virtuous Revolutionary* (Baton Rouge: Louisiana State University Press, 1981), p. 125. The same year Almon published Lee's *Answer to Considerations on Certain Political Transactions of the Province of South Carolina*. According to Jack Greene, this pamphlet was financed by Henry Laurens and Ralph Izard. See the introduction to Greene, ed., *The Nature of Colony Constitutions: Two Pamphlets on the Wilkes Fund Controversy in South Carolina by Sir Egerton Leigh and Arthur Lee* (South Carolina: University of South Carolina Press, 1970), p. 40.

[13] William B. Willcox, ed., *The Papers of Benjamin Franklin* (New Haven: Yale University Press, 1978), XXI, 372; *Memoirs*, p. 92.

[14] Willcox, ed., XXI, 372.

[15] *Memoirs*, p. 92. Franklin may have convinced his associate Thomas Paine to deal with Almon, who published the inflamatory anonymous work that the London press widely attributed to Franklin, Paine's *Common Sense* (Printed in Philadelphia in 1776 and reprinted in London for Almon the same year). See Solomon Lutnick, *The American Revolution and the British Press 1775–1783* (Missouri: University of Missouri Press, 1967), pp. 45–46 and Paine's letter to Franklin of 20 June 1777.

[16] Willcox, ed., XXI, 450–53. Earlier, Franklin may have provided Almon with the text for his edition of *Extracts from the Votes and Proceedings of the American Continental Congress* (1775). See Willcox, ed., XXI, 390–91.

[17] In her letter to Walter King of 4 July 1779, Burke's wife, Jane, pointed directly to Almon as the Burkes' source of information: ". . . as to News we must learn that from you, for your Duke [Richmond] will be able to tell you more than the repository in Piccadilly, can inform us." See John Woods, ed., *The Correspondence of Edmund Burke* (Chicago: University of Chicago Press, 1963), IV, 97–98.

There is also some evidence that Almon was friendly with William Burke, who was extremely close to his cousin Edmund (Cone, p. 289). Here it should be noted that Almon had previously attempted to provoke Burke by publishing William Knox's *Present State of the Nation* (1768), which supported George Grenville and attacked the Rockingham faction. According to Cone (p. 173), Almon published this tract in an apparent attempt to excite a response from the Rockingham Whigs. We can gain some understanding of the way in which Almon conducted business from Knox's letters to Grenville. In his letter of 4 October 1768 Knox described Almon's tactics for distributing his pamphlet:

> Almon has general orders from a great number of Members of Parliament to send them whatever comes out in the recess, and he intends taking the opportunity of the intervening fortnight, between meetings at Newmarket, to

convey this pamphlet to them. He thinks of sending one elegantly done up to the King, as he has done with some other such matters. He is an excellent fellow at circulating a work, and understands all the mystery of raising its character, and exciting purchasers (*Grenville Papers*, IV, 368–69).

On 18 October 1769, evidently referring to the new edition Almon published in this year, Knox gave a similar account of Almon's strategy:

Almon, who is a thorough judge of times and seasons for publication, does not intend to publish it 'till the return from Newmarket races, which will be the week after next, when many persons from different parts of the kingdom pass through London. In the meantime he sends it to all those who leave orders with him for every new thing (*Grenville Papers*, IV, 469; 470–73).

Almon's success in promoting this work may be measured by the response. Knox's tract inspired no less a work than Burke's *Observations on a Late State of the Nation* (1769). On behalf of the Rockingham camp, Burke wrote his famous answer to Knox's pamphlet.

[18] *Memoirs*, pp. 93–94; George H. Guttridge, ed., *The Correspondence of Edmund Burke* (Chicago: University of Chicago Press, 1961), III, 184. Another of Almon's correspondents, John Lloyd (whom I have been unable to identify), expressed his concern with the fate of the petition in his letter to Almon of 21 September 1775 (Add. MS. 20733 fos. 67–68).

[19] Guttridge, ed., III, 233.

[20] *The Letters of Valens* (London: Printed for J. Almon, 1777). Earlier Almon had published a work written by Burke (possibly with John Christopher Roberts and William Mellish), *A True History of A Late Short Administration* (1766; rpt. London: J. Almon, 1766).

[21] Almon, *Biographical . . . Anecdotes . . .* , II, 347. (For Almon's account of the Burkes, see pp. 345–73.) According to Guttridge, ed., III, 233, these letters are now thought to be the work of William Burke. William Todd, however, on the basis of Almon's attribution, assigns this work to all three Burkes. See *A Bibliography of Edmund Burke* (London: Hart-Davis, 1964), pp. 86–87. Here Todd persuasively argues that Almon "at the time of printing must have had personal knowledge of the contributors, since he then accepted from them a text varying from that originally represented in the newspaper."

[22] Add. MS. 20733 fo. 57.

[23] See also Woods, ed., IV, 42. Burke and other members of the Rockingham faction warmly backed Keppel, who was acquitted. Almon's support for Keppel is reflected in many of the letters found among his papers in the British Library (Add. MS. 20733 fos. 12–13, 16, 61, 63, 127, and 155).

[24] *An Authentic and Impartial Copy of the Trial of the Hon. Augustus Keppel* was printed in Portsmouth and sold in London by Wheldon.

[25] Todd, pp. 93–96. *The Defence of Admiral Keppel* was printed in London for John Almon in 1779. Simultaneously Almon issued *The Proceedings at Large of the Court-Martial*. If Burke's letter to Almon of April, 1779 is any indication, he often sent other business Almon's way:

The gentleman who delivers this to you, is a friend to the author of the pamphlet, which accompanies it. As far as I am capable of judging, the subject is handled with a very considerable degree of ability; and though the opinions, toward the latter end, differ a good deal from mine, the public I think may profit by the discussion of them. How far it may suit you in the way of trade, you can best judge; or how far the public is or is not satiated with this sort of speculation. On these matters, I ought rather to take your opinion, than to attempt to lead you by any of mine, as the author is wholly unknown to me (*Memoirs*, p. 113).

The date of this letter has been called into question by R. B. McDowell and John Woods, ed., *The Correspondence of Edmund Burke* (Chicago: University of Chicago Press, 1970), IX, 429–30. The identity of the pamphlet and its author remain unknown.

[26] Woods, ed., IV, 175. (See also Todd, pp. 97–98.)

[27] Woods suggests that Burke supplied Almon with the copy (IV, 175).

[28] The following year, Almon published *The Yorkshire Question*, which he attributed to Edmund, William, and Richard Burke (Todd, p. 98). This pamphlet argued against increasing the power of the Crown and curbing the freedom of the press. In addition, in 1783 John Debrett, Almon's successor, published a House of Commons report that was drawn up by Burke, the *Ninth Report from the Select Committee* (Todd, 41d–9).

[29] Woods, ed., IV, 175.

[30] Besides those publications previously mentioned, some of the other pro-American works Almon published (listed chronologically) include: John Dickinson, *The Late Regulations Respecting the British Colonies on the Continent of America Considered* [Printed in Philadelphia in 1765 and reprinted for Almon the same year. Almon issued a second edition in 1766; Sabin 20043. See also entries 10b and 10c in Thomas R. Adams, *American Independence the Growth of an Idea* (Providence: Brown University Press, 1965), hereafter cited as Adams], as well as Dickinson's *Letters from a Farmer in Pennsylvania, to the Inhabitants of the British Colonies* (Printed in Boston in 1768 and reprinted in London for Almon the same year); *An Address to the People of England* (London: Printed for the author and sold by J. Almon, 1766; *American Controversy* 66–1); *The Adventure of a Bale of Goods from America, in Consequence of the Stamp Act* (London: Printed for J. Almon, 1766; *American Controversy* 66–2); Daniel Dulany, *Considerations on the Propriety of Imposing Taxes in the British Colonies* (Originally printed in America, this tract went through at least four editions from 1765–66 before Almon published the first English edition in 1766. Another edition was printed for Almon the same year; Sabin 21170; Adams 11f and 11g); Stephen Hopkins, *The Grievances of the American Colonies Candidly Examined* (Printed in Providence in 1765 and reprinted for Almon in 1766; Sabin 32967; Adams 14b); *The Necessity of Repealing the American Stamp-Act Demonstrated . . .* (1766; Sabin 52213; Adams 38a); James Otis, *A Vindication of the British Colonies* (Printed in Boston in 1765 and reprinted in London for Almon in 1769; see Brewer, pp. 215–16); *Observations on Several Acts of Parliament . . . by the Merchants of Boston* [London: J. Almon, 1770; see William B. Willcox, ed., *The Papers of Benjamin Franklin* (New Haven: Yale University Press, 1972), XVI, 272–73]; *Report on the Lords Commissioners for Trade and Plantations on the Petition of the Honourable Thomas Walpole, Benjamin Franklin, John Sargent, and Samuel Wharton . . . for a Grant of Lands on the River Ohio . . . for the Purpose of Erecting a New Government . . .* (London: Printed for J. Almon, 1772; see *Biographical . . . Anecdotes*, II, 200–322); John Cartwright, *Take your Choice!* (London: Printed for J. Almon, 1776; *American Controversy* 76–18a and b); *A Letter to Lord George Germaine* (London: J. Almon, 1776); Thomas O'Beirne, *Candid and Impartial Narrative of the Transactions of the Fleet under the Command of Lord Howe . . .* [London: J. Almon, 1779; see

entry 4 in Kenneth Nebenzahl, *A Bibliography of Printed Battle Plans of the American Revolution 1775–1795* (Chicago: University of Chicago Press, 1975)]; Thomas Pownall, *The Right, Interest, and Duty, of Government* (1773; rpt. London: Printed for J. Almon, 1781; *American Controversy* 73–11b).

Almon also edited several collections of documents related to the American Revolution. (These compilations include many of the tracts listed above.) For example, in 1766 Almon published *A Collection of the Most Interesting Tracts, Lately Published in England and America, on the Subjects of Taxing the American Colonies, and Regulating their Trade* (2 vols.; Sabin 952, 14392, 34901. For a description of the contents, see *American Controversy* 66–3 and 66–4). The following year Almon published a third volume of the *Collection* (described in *American Controversy* 67–1). And in 1773 he compiled *A Collection of Tracts, on the Subjects of Taxing the British Colonies in America and Regulating their Trade. In Four Volumes* (*American Controversy* 73–1). For more of Almon's publications concerning America, consult appendix.

[31] For example, in his letter from Philadelphia of 20 March 1779, Thomas Bradford sought to establish such a relationship with Almon:

> As a printer, I need not expatiate on the mutual benefit of an exchange of newpapers: I have therefore taken the liberty to send you a number of mine, and request the favour of yours, by such opportunities as may offer. . . . I shall continue to send you my papers; and if you think they are not adequate to yours, please to open an account against me, and it shall be punctually paid, as soon as a communication is open between England and America.
>
> I must also beg you will send me the Parliamentary Debates, and all other publications interesting to Americans, which shall be thankfully paid for as above. If an epistolary correspondence on the news and transactions of the states of Europe, would be safe and agreeable to you, I shall be glad to hear from you as lengthy as you please; and you may depend on my giving you, from time to time, the best intelligence the country affords (*Memoirs*, pp. 111–12).

[32] Thomas Pownall may have helped Almon with the editing. See John Nichols, *Literary Anecdotes of the Eighteenth Century* (London: Printed for the author by Nichols, son, and Bentley, 1814), VIII, 63. Almon also published a compilation entitled *A Collection of Interesting, Authentic Papers, Relative to the Dispute between Great Britain and America; Shewing the Causes and Progress of that Misunderstanding, from 1764 to 1775* (1777; Sabin 951; *American Controversy* 71–13). Usually cited as "Prior Documents," it was intended to accompany *The Remembrancer*.

During this period Almon was also concerned with establishing the *London Courant*, which we need not consider here since his precise relationship with this paper, which is difficult to assess, has been taken up at length by Lucyle Werkmeister (pp. 119–31). Almon apparently edited the *Courant*, which was, for the most part, a vehicle for advertising, from its inception in 1779 until Almon's retirement in 1781.

[33] Almon as quoted in *Public Characters*, p. 134. Even if political and commercial concerns dictated the nature of Almon's productions, his historical approach (luckily enough for us) made him preoccupied with the preservation of ephemera, from fugitive pieces to parliamentary records. The very existence of such material today demonstrates Almon's success.

[34] For example, on 20 March 1779, Samuel Wharton, an American land developer, wrote to Almon from Paris:

I wish to give you some American papers for your Remembrancer, and if I thought, you would not lose them, Through the Infidelity of the Post Office, I would immediately send them;—perhaps I may venture to forward them, notwithstanding the Expence of the postage, by this Conveyance. I shall be obliged to you to favour me with any News of *Importance*, that may from time to time arrive in your City; as you may know there is no kind of dependence to be placed in Newspaper Intelligence. You may depend upon my forwarding the American Newspapers, as soon as I can get them and always upon my Friendship. . .

(Add. MS. 20733 fo. 112).

[35] In addition to those letters already cited, see Add. MS. 20733 fos. 57, 59, 61, 67, 69, 71, 73, 75, 77, 78, 115, 127, 138, 140, 143, and 148.

[36] Add. MS. 20733 fos. 59–60.

[37] Add. MS. 20733 fos. 67–68.

[38] Add. MS. 20733 fo. 70.

[39] Add. MS. 20733 fo. 71.

[40] Several days later Almon received another letter lamenting the situation in Canada and surmising that there had been British losses in the South. It is endorsed on the front "Frm Mr Izard":

[I] . . . am sorry to have had so sudden a damper as the total evacuation of Canada. . . . The Ministry must have heard something from the Southern Provinces . . . & as the Gazette is silent about any new crop of Laurels, possibly their Heroes in that part of the Continent may have given them no cause to sing Te Deum (4 August 1776; Add. MS. 20733 fos. 57–58).

[41] Add. MS. 20733 fo. 73.

[42] On 17 October 1776 (Add. MS. 20733 fo. 77), Lloyd sent Almon a revised impression:

The last post a friend informed me that by way of France he has just received a letter from Philadelphia dated the beginning of August which mentioned that the Congress were unanimous in the determination to adhere to their declaration of Independency. . . . That the people at large were resolved to endure with patience every hardship rather than submit to a re-union—That thousands had offered to march to New York, whenever there should be occasion. That they had received such vast supplies of Military Stores, that the Congress had requested the Merchants to import no more—

[43] Add. MS. 20733 fo. 75.

[44] Add. MS. 20733 fo. 77. This must have been particularly interesting to Almon, who later criticized the ministry for hiring German troops in his *Political Paradox* (London: Printed for J. Almon, 1777; Sabin 63792; *American Controversy* 77–14).

[45] Add. MS. 20733 fo. 78.

[46] Sykes's letter is dated 30 March 1778 from Liverpool (Add. MS. 20733 fo. 123).

[47] Add. MS. 20733 fos. 126–27.

[48] Here Sykes may have been referring to John Kennion's letter to Almon of 12 October 1778 (Add. MS. 20733 fo. 61).

[49] Among the Almon papers in the New-York Historical Society is a receipt for 105 pounds for the full purchase of a house at Box Moor (fo. 30), which was probably used as an investment since Almon appears to have built his own house. See also Add. MS. 20733 fo. 101.

[50] Obituary, *Gentleman's Magazine*, p. 1179; *Memoirs*, p. 121. There is some evidence that Stockdale may have also been involved (Werkmeister, pp. 122–23). In any event, as early as 1780, Debrett's name began to appear with Almon's on his imprint. For 1781 the imprint on publications issued by the shop at 178 Piccadilly varies. Some works were "Printed for J. Almon and J. Debrett"; some were "Printed for J. Debrett (successor to Mr. Almon)," while others were printed for multiple booksellers. In the years to follow, Almon's name would often continue to accompany Debrett's.

[51] Rea, "Bookseller as Historian," pp. 82–83; Maxted, p. 3.

[52] Untitled poem by Almon in *New Foundling*, III, 266.

[53] *Ibid.*, III, 266.

[54] *Memoirs*, p. 122.

[55] [John Almon] "On the Death of _____," in *New Foundling*, III, 264.

[56] Altered from Rowe (Almon's note).

[57] "Epitaph," in *New Foundling*, III, 263.

[58] "To Mr. Sykes," in *New Foundling*, III, 265.

[59] *Memoirs*, pp. 122–23.

6
Last Years

In September, 1784, Almon returned to London and established his business at 183 Fleet Street.[1] The specific occasion for this move was his marriage to the widow of William Parker, who had been printer and owner of the *General Advertiser*.[2] It is more than likely that Almon married for financial reasons. On the whole, his contemporaries simply assumed that his second marriage was little more than a good business arrangement. According to Almon's obituary in the *Gentleman's Magazine*, ". . . the death of Mr. Parker, the printer of the General Advertiser, opened a new scene for his talents and his ambition" (p. 1179). William Jackson, who attacked Almon's motives for his remarriage in the *Morning Post* of 16 and 20 October 1784, put the matter in harsher terms, observing that Almon "only thought of matrimony to better his fortune."[3] From Almon himself, we hear almost nothing about his new wife.[4]

There were other changes: Almon served as a councilman from 1784 to 1786, once again fully participating in London life.[5] Lucyle Werkmeister (pp. 131–49), relying on what little evidence exists, has attempted to trace Almon's activities from this point until 1793 (about the time her book ends), tentatively reconstructing his association with the *General Advertiser* from details that surface in the paper itself, in Almon's *Memoirs*, and in William Jackson's exposés.[6] Werkmeister's research may be briefly summarized.

Upon taking over control of the *General Advertiser* in 1784, Almon conducted the paper with a view toward courting both Government and Opposition and receiving subsidies from both. For a time, Almon seems to have accepted money from whatever source it came. It is hard to believe that Almon's double-dealing could have remained a closely guarded secret. In any event, William Jackson's attacks in the *Morning Post* left no doubt of Almon's duplicity. According to Jackson, several months before acquiring the *General Advertiser*, Almon had been writing for the Treasury in support of the Pitt administration. Upon assuming charge of the paper, however, Almon attempted to serve both political parties. In such a situation, it was not long before Almon was forced to choose sides: By publishing two libels on William Pitt the younger in the *General Advertiser* (20 and 27 October 1786), Almon announced his support for the Opposition.[7] Although Pitt sued Almon for 150,000 pounds and Almon was, in fact, technically convicted, his fine was reduced to 150 pounds, a comparatively small sum.[8]

Almon's probable aim in libelling Pitt was to ingratiate himself with Charles James Fox. In this he was successful, and from 1787–89, he received subsidies from the Foxite Whigs. Taking their part by arguing for the Prince of Wales's claims to an immediate Regency, Almon again found himself facing a trial for libel in 1788. At issue were remarks concerning the King's insanity that had appeared in the *General Advertiser* (18 November 1788). The political thrust of Almon's trial was, once more, unmistakable. Almon was prosecuted and, when he failed to appear for sentencing, outlawed. In short order, he sold his paper, declared bankruptcy, and fled from London. Almon's whereabouts and movements from 1789 until 1792 are uncertain. Although Werkmeister allows that he may have left for France, she finds it more likely that he remained in Box Moor. These conclusions, however, would presumably be altered if Werkmeister were aware of an autograph draft of a letter dated 7 March 1791, where Almon maintained that it was "not prudent that he be publicly seen in London therefore since my return to England I keep to the country. . . ."[9]

During this period Almon wrote his anecdotes of Chatham, which he had apparently undertaken to appease the younger Pitt.[10] Something of a fugitive until the publication of this work,

Almon surrendered and was imprisoned in the King's Bench from March, 1792 to April, 1793, when his outlawry charge was reversed.

One would obviously like to have more evidence about Almon's life during these years, but an extensive search through the files of contemporary newspapers and through Almon's manuscripts has turned up little beyond what Werkmeister has already discovered. Although Almon's autobiography supplies an account of his activities until 1790, the year it was published, since Almon in all probability wrote this work to ingratiate himself with the Government, he is honest and direct concerning matters already of public record, but evasive where it suits his purposes. The final chapters are at times especially unreliable. This is presumably because Almon wrote his *Memoirs* when he was being sought as an outlaw, and revealing specific information would have been dangerous. Although Almon lived for another fifteen years after the publication of his *Memoirs*, in the absence of records, it is difficult to establish, with any degree of certainty, the events during the last part of his life.

Even though considerable ambiguity attends almost everything that occurred during this period, it seems that Almon's imprisonment was the principal cause of his subsequent withdrawal. He spent his remaining years in Box Moor, never again to resume his bookselling and printing activities. (Perhaps the change was inevitable since Almon had sold his business.) Moreover, if we examine his later works, it seems as if he also withdrew from the current political scene and turned his thoughts to earlier concerns. Although Almon still maintained an interest in politics, his chief productions during this time were his *Biographical, Literary, and Political Anecdotes* and his editions of Wilkes and of Junius.

Issued in three volumes in 1797, Almon's anecdotes featured previously unpublished pieces on such friends, acquaintances, and enemies as Lords Temple, Grafton, Camden, and Mansfield. Also included were sketches of Josiah Wedgwood, Edmund Burke, Benjamin Franklin, David Hartley, Charles

Townshend, and George Grenville. As a signed autograph draft of his letter to George Chalmers, the Scottish antiquarian, indicates, Almon prided himself on the accuracy of this work:

> I feel some satisfaction, that in three volumes of Anecdotes, not published before, concerning the ministers of the present reign, the truth of only *one* of them has been doubted; and this after the most minute enquiry, and the most strict scrutiny, is believed to be well-founded. . . .[11]

During this period Almon also compiled the first complete collection of Wilkes's letters. (See above.) All evidence suggests that Almon must have worked at breakneck speed, since he had reason to believe that a rival edition was at least being contemplated. This is apparent from two drafts of Almon's letters in the New-York Historical Society. The first, dated 6 September 1804, is an attempt to discourage Captain Dardis, a potential competitor. To judge from Almon's letter, Dardis seems to have written to Richard Phillips, who was to publish Almon's edition, about several letters ostensibly from Wilkes that were unknown to Almon:

> I have seen your applications to M[r] Phillips your letter of Sept[r] 3 is now before me. It is impossible to say any thing respecting the letters without seeing them. You say they are integral may be so but upon what subject. I never heard lord Temple mention them. . . . I should be sorry to see my work perplexed by another & therefore wish to avoid it or to enter into any public disputation which two publications will certainly create consequently Sir I shall be glad to see you on the subject and if you will be so good to honour with a note informing me when I may meet you in Pall Mall I will go to London for that purpose giving me 2 or 3 notice for the post here is not very regular. . . .[12]

The second of these drafts, written several weeks later, is an attempt to reassure Phillips and, at the same time, stress the importance of speedy publication. By the time the draft of his letter was written, part of Almon's edition was already in press:

I received your letter of the 19th by yesterday's post. I am sorry to observe that you seem to be much alarmed. . . . I will see you in the first week in October. I thank you sir very sincerely for the polite offer of residence at your house but it is natural to me to prefer my daughter's House. On Wednesday next I shall send the 4th vol to London. The fifth I shall postpone until I have finished the first which will require much attention & which I hope to bring with me. Pray hurry the printers as much as you can. Much depends on their dispatch. . . . Pray order your printers to send no more proofs. The copy is clear enough for any blockhead to read. . . .[13]

His edition of Wilkes finished, Almon began his next and final project, which was in keeping with his retrospective temperament towards the end of his life.[14] Indeed, it seems wholly fitting that, embarking on his last venture, Almon, who had published one of the first (obviously incomplete) collections of the Junius letters near the beginning of his career, should return to compile a complete edition of the notorious satirist.[15]

Like so many others of his day, Almon attempted to identify Junius, whom he vigorously, if incorrectly, contended was the Irish essayist, Hugh Macaulay Boyd.[16] The difficulty with Almon's argument lies primarily in the circumstantiality of his evidence. It seems that one night in October, 1769, Henry Sampson Woodfall, publisher of the *Public Advertiser*, the paper where the letters were first printed, read a Junius letter to a gathering of fellow booksellers, which included Almon. Upon accidentally catching sight of several pages of the letter, Almon became convinced that the handwriting bore a striking resemblance to that of Hugh Boyd. Almon was quick to confront Boyd, whose embarrassed reaction he took to constitute proof.[17]

However extravagant Almon's theory may have been, it had its supporters. For example, George Chalmers voiced a similar conviction in *An Appendix to the Supplemental Apology to the Believers in the Suppositious Shakespeare-Papers: being the Documents for the Opinion that Hugh McAuley Boyd Wrote Junius's Letters* (London: T. Egerton, 1800). In the draft of a letter for the

Morning Post which is addressed to Chalmers and dated 25 August 1800, Almon acknowledged his authorship of an early item that named Boyd as Junius:

> You say this mystery was *first* revealed (that Mr Boyd was the writer of Junius's letters) in a paragraph in the General Advertiser in April 1786, which alarmed Mrs Boyd very much, &c as neither Mrs Boyd, nor Mr Almon, sent that paragraph, it follows *from the fact,* that some other person suspected Boyd to be the writer of Junius. Of this mistake you might have corrected yourself; if you had read a little further in my letter . . . you would have found these words, Mr Boyd was "not at that time suspected, I believe, by anybody, except myself." This plainly informs you *who* wrote the paragraph.[18]

Almon then addressed Chalmers' contention that William Gerard ("Single Speech") Hamilton was not talented enough to have written the Junius letters. Almon's response was grounded first and foremost in his relationship with Hamilton and "the many conversations with which Mr Hamilton was pleased to honour me during upwards of twenty years close friendship":

> As to Mr Hamilton not being the writer of Junius's letters I might have said so from my own knowledge of Mr Hamilton, for I believe that no person, during that period, was more in Mr Hamilton's confidence, respecting his literary & political pursuits. . . . You say Mr Hamilton was not the writer of Junius's letters because *you think* he was "incapable of writing them." If the word "incapable" applies to Mr Hamilton's Talents, I will not indeed be so rude to give it a flat contradiction, but I will say that the opinion is formed upon a very imperfect knowledge of Mr Hamilton. Some of that Gentleman's compositions in the years 1769 and 1770 were carried to the foot of the throne. If I were at liberty to point them out, able & candid judges would say, they are equal if not superior to any of the productions of either Mr Burke or Mr Boyd.

Almon went on to defend Hamilton from the charge that Samuel Johnson had a part in his writings:

Nor can I give credit to your story of Mr Hamilton soliciting the literary assistance of the late Dr. Johnson. Johnson was a mad Tory, a pensioner, and the slave of faction. Mr Hamilton was strongly attached to Lord Temple, and if that noble lord could have accepted the Treasury (which was repeatedly offered to him) with honour to himself, Mr Hamilton was to have been his chancellor of the Exchequer. It would be supposing a great deal too much, to suppose that Mr Hamilton was so weak a man as to shew Johnson his papers. He must know very little of Mr Hamilton who can believe he wanted any "literary help" as you call it (page 14) from Johnson.[19]

In further support of his argument, Almon gave one of Hamilton's anecdotes about Johnson, which is of special interest since it is the earliest preserved version of this incident:[20]

> Mr Hamilton used to relate the following anecdote of Johnson. Count Holke, who accompanied the King of Denmark to England in the year 1768, was induced by the fame of Johnson, to pay him a visit; which lasted some hours. Count Holke was so exceedingly disgusted and disappointed in Johnson, that he said so shallow a fellow he had never met with. It is not probable that Mr Hamilton would tell this story of his preceptor.

From the draft of a letter now preserved at the New-York Historical Society, it appears that Almon was also concerned to prove that General Charles Lee was not Junius.[21] Whatever the reasons for the original claim (which do not appear), Almon's argument set forth two principal points. The first involved the relationship between Wilkes and Lee: ". . . the strongest proof of all is Lee & Wilkes had never any acquaintance. Lee was patronized by 1^d S[andwich] and W[ilkes] was hated by S." Almon's second point involved chronology: "In 1772 Boyd went to Ireland until 1779. . . . Junius ceased to write in Jan 72 Lee did not begin to write until autumn 74 He was then just come from America." These arguments do not seem wholly satisfactory. Although Almon may adequately demonstrate that Lee was not Junius, it is unclear how such reasoning would distinguish Junius from countless friends of Wilkes who were writing prior to January, 1772. Indeed, there is no little irony in the fact that the case advanced in this letter would not eliminate Almon himself.

Basing his work on Woodfall's edition of 1772 (with several additions, mostly of letters to which Junius had responded), Almon edited, annotated, and wrote a preliminary essay for his collection of the letters, which he must have completed shortly before his death. Almon did not live to see the publication of his edition. At Box Moor on 12 December 1805, John Almon died at the age of sixty-eight, remaining to the end shrouded in enigma.

Notes

[1] William Todd, *A Directory of Printers and Others in Allied Trades, London and Vicinity 1800-1840* (London: Printing Historical Society, 1972), p. 3; Maxted, p. 3. Todd lists Almon as a printer at this address from 1784 to 1790, when he moved to 182 Fleet Street (p. 3). That Almon was engaged as a printer is consistent with his early training. Moreover, when Almon sold the *General Advertiser*, he was "obliged to dispose of his paper, and *printing materials*" (*Memoirs*, p. 143; emphasis added). Although printers' names were often omitted from eighteenth-century imprints, from 1783 to 1792, Almon's name (unaccompanied by Debrett's) does appear several times as printer or printer-publisher. See entires in appendix for Galloway, Lennox, Lonsdale, MacNally (2), Mellish, Morres, O'Bryen, Pilon (2), *Report of the Lords of the Committee of Council*. On previous imprints, Almon's name is usually given solely as publisher except in several instances from 1772 to 1780, where he is listed as printer or printer-publisher. See appendix under Baillie, Bollan (5), Burke, Graham, Greenwood, and Hope.

[2] Almon started paying the advertisement duty on the *General Advertiser* in 1785 (Aspinall, "Statistical Accounts," p. 226).

[3] Jackson as quoted by Werkmeister, p. 132.

[4] In his *Memoirs* (p. 125), Almon mentions her only once (and in passing).

[5] Maxted, p. 3; *Memoirs*, pp. 127–31. Almon represented the Ward of Farringdon Without in the City Senate (Obituary, *Gentleman's Magazine*, p. 1180). There is also some evidence that Almon may have started the *Sunday Chronicle* (Werkmeister, p. 139; Maxted, p. 3).

[6] Jackson's articles appeared in the *Morning Post*, a ministerial paper, throughout September and October, 1784.

[7] Almon's offending paragraphs criticized Pitt for selling false stocks on the occasion of the Dutch peace.

[8] The Almon collection at the New-York Historical Society (fo. 73) contains the following receipt for court costs:

> 18th May 1786   Received of John Almon Esquire the Sum of Twenty eight pounds thirteen shillings in full for the Bill of Costs in the Cause of the

Honorable William Pitt against Mr Almon deducting nine pounds and six shillings the Amount of M^r. Almon's Account against me.

Geo Broome
for Mr Reynolds

⁹ NYHS MS. fo. 89. The likelihood that Almon was abroad at least part of this time is increased if we can regard seriously the attributive subtitle of a work Almon completed, the *History of France, from the Most Early Records, to the Death of Louis XVI: The Ancient Part by William Beckford. . . .the Modern Part by an English Gentleman, who has been some time Resident in Paris*, 4 vols. (London: J.S. Jordan, 1794).

¹⁰ For a description of Almon's *Anecdotes of the Life of the Right Hon. William Pitt, Earl of Chatham*, which was published in two volumes by J.S. Jordan in early 1792, see Rea, "Bookseller as Historian," pp. 84–87.

¹¹ NYHS MS. fo. 2 (25 August 1800). The Almon collection in the New-York Historical Society also contains a draft of Almon's letter to Grafton of 2 March 1798 (fo. 29). Here Almon's mention of the Whittlewood anecdote is of more than casual interest. Junius had attacked the Duke of Grafton for asserting that his appointment as ranger of Whittlewood Forest gave him the right to its timber. Although Grafton could not exercise this right by virtue of his position, a previous patent, which Junius ignored, had granted him the underwood [For further details concerning this dispute, see W.H. Hart, "Letters of Junius," *Notes and Queries*, 3rd ser., VIII (1865), 230–33 and my response, "The Whittlewood Controversy," *Notes and Queries*, NS 31 (1984), 407]:

> Accidently meeting M^r [Alexander] Annesley in the street in the course of a little conversation commenced in his usual kindness he mentioned Your Grace's approbation of the state of the timber in Whittlebury given in the work entitled Biographical & Political Anecdotes I was very happy to hear this intelligence & beg leave to assure your Grace my motive in this & other particulars was a sincere wish to undeceive the public in cases of great misrepresentation & I think few persons have been so much misrepresented as Your Grace. If my materials had been better my earnest endeavours would have kept pace with them.

As in many of his letters, Almon referred to his poor health:

> An indifferent state of health prevents my residing in London. Therefore I date this letter from my son's house in Coventry Street. Permit me to offer your Grace my humble thanks for the approbation you have been pleased to express. . . .

¹² NYHS MS. fo. 84.

¹³ NYHS MS. fo. 85 (21 September 1804).

¹⁴ For further details concerning Almon's editions of Wilkes and of Junius, see Rea, "Bookseller as Historian."

¹⁵ Almon's *Collection of the Letters of Atticus, Lucius, and Junius* appeared in 1769. Although Francesco Cordasco's scholarship is often suspect, entires 21–23 and 31 in his *Junius Bibliography* (1949; rpt. New York: Burt Franklin, 1974) may be consulted for a description of this work. For Almon's *Letters of Junius* (London: Richard Phillips, 1806), see Cordasco 102. Cordasco also cites works that include references to Almon (entries 172–79, 184, 188–91, 214, 241, 388, 538).

¹⁶ Although there have been various attempts to discover who Junius was, to this day his identity remains a mystery. The many candidates who have been advanced over

the years include (among others) Edmund Burke, Hugh Boyd, Edward Gibbon, Philip Francis, William Hamilton, George Grenville, John Wilkes, Thomas Paine, John Horne Tooke, Horace Walpole, and Lords Sackville, Portland, Chatham, and Chesterfield (McCracken, p. 19). Even if everything now points to Philip Francis, there is still room for disagreement. As late as 1974, Cordasco claimed that Junius was an obscure Irishman named Lauchlin Macleane (*Junius Bibliography*, p. xii).

[17] Almon's argument appears in the preface to his 1806 edition.

[18] NYHS MS. fo. 2. See also Almon's *Free Parliaments* (London: Printed for J. Debrett, 1783), p. 62, where Almon hints at the identification between Boyd and Junius.

[19] Despite Almon's contentions, there is reason to believe that Johnson did in fact assist Hamilton in such a manner. For example, in 1755 Thomas Birch insisted that Johnson had composed Hamilton's first (and only) speech in Parliament. See E.L. McAdam, Jr., with Donald and Mary Hyde, ed., *Samuel Johnson: Diaries, Prayers, and Annals* (New Haven: Yale University Press, 1958), I, 98.

Basing his information about Almon solely on the DNB, Donald Greene takes issue with this entire account. See my "Newer Light on Johnson," *Johnsonian News Letter*, XLIII, Nos. 1–2 (1983), 13–14 and Greene's reply in Nos. 3–4, pp. 7–8. Some of Hamilton's letters to Almon may be found in the *Memoirs*, pp. 102–103.

[20] Three years later, an embellished version appeared in *The Monthly Magazine*, XV (1803), 151. This report may have been derived from Almon's account, since *The Monthly Magazine* was then being published by Richard Phillips.

[21] Almon's draft, dated 22 September 1805, is directed to Richard Phillips, who was to publish his edition of the satirist (NYHS MS. fo. 19).

Afterword

In this biographical study of Almon's career, no attempt has been made to evaluate his life psychologically, for this would have involved speculating beyond the available evidence. There are clearly shades of mystery that still cling to Almon, despite new, unpublished material to which the present writer has had access. Looking back over Almon's endeavors, however, one is necessarily struck by the impact of politics on his output. From the start, Almon's relationship with Richard Grenville, Earl Temple, was a shaping force: If Temple funded Almon, in turn, Almon supported him on every issue. Within a short period of time, Temple helped Almon establish his own (heavily subsidized) business, which would soon catapult Almon to fame as the leading political publisher of his day. Their arrangement committed Almon to promote Opposition literature and introduced a situation in which politics directly influenced both Almon and his publications.

Another consequence of Almon's connection with Temple was his acquaintance with John Wilkes. As Wilkes became increasingly radical, a corresponding change took place in Almon, whose encouragement of Wilkes manifested itself in various ways: Not only was Almon prosecuted for publishing *A Letter Concerning Libels*, he provided Wilkes with a vehicle for publicity, the *Political Register*, which contributed largely to the Wilkite cause.

Throughout this period the works Almon wrote and/or published were informed by the political attitudes of Temple and of Wilkes. But in 1770, when legal constraints made it difficult for him to produce such factional material, Almon, at least for the moment, turned primarily to literary modes as an alternative outlet for political expression. The change in

107

Almon's publications under these conditions dramatically corroborates the theory already proposed: Political repression had a significant effect on Almon's career. Although he published comparatively little that was politically sensitive during this period, Almon's role in the Printers' Case and his correspondence with John Calcraft testify to the fact that, in spite of his problems with the law, Almon never abandoned his interest in politics.

By the time Almon was able fully to resume publication of controversial works, his primary interest had become the developing dispute between England and America. To judge how extensive a role Almon played in promoting the cause of the colonies, one has only to examine his business transactions with Edmund Burke and with Benjamin Franklin and his pro-American publications. Especially as the editor of the *Remembrancer*, Almon helped to disseminate American propaganda. A further mark of Almon's interest in the events concerning America is his vast correspondence regarding the Revolution.

Meanwhile, events had taken a turn. After temporarily retiring from business for personal reasons, Almon assumed control of the *General Advertiser* in 1784. Here again, he encountered political difficulties, but this time, with greater consequences. Almon's alliance with Charles James Fox not only governed the perspective of the *General Advertiser*, it eventually forced him out of business and led to his imprisonment and complete withdrawal from the contemporary political scene.

In arriving at a final evaluation of Almon's career, I have tried to record without exaggeration the way in which political considerations dictated the nature of what was issued under his imprint. Through the study of this now obscure bookseller, we can gain some appreciation of an important aspect of eighteenth-century publishing history. But a final problem remains. It is difficult to estimate the extent to which Almon's life and work were typical of other publishers and, perhaps more significantly, the extent of which political pressures on booksellers affected the literature of the period.

Bibliography

Manuscript Sources

Almon, John. British Library Add. MS. 20733; Add. MS. 38728 fo. 194; Add. MS. 38730 fo. 10; Add. MS. 32939 fo. 242; Add. MS. 32959 fo. 233; Add. MS. 30868 fos. 136–37; Add. MS. 30869 fos. 95, 106–107, 110, 119, 123, 128, 139, 144, 151, 153, 157; Add. MS. 30870 fo. 107; Add. MS. 30875 fo. 4.
Almon, John. New-York Historical Society MS.
Almon, John. William R. Perkins Library of Duke University MS. XVIII-E.
Public Record Office. Treasury Board, Treasury Soliticor Papers No. 765 and Audit Office and Pipe Office Papers, Accounts, Various, Nos. 1398–99.

Primary Sources

An Address to the People of England Shewing the Advantages Arising from the Frequent Changes of Ministers with an Address to the Next Administration. London: Printed for the author and sold by J. Almon, 1766.
The Adventure of a Bale of Goods from America, in Consequence of the Stamp Act. London: Printed for J. Almon, 1766.
Almon, John. *An Address to the Interior Cabinet on the Affairs of America.* London: Debrett, 1782.
_____. *Anecdotes of the Life of the Right Hon. William Pitt, Earl of Chatham.* 2. vols. London: J.S. Jordan, 1792.
_____. *An Appendix to the Review of Mr. Pitt's Administration by the Author of the Review.* London: J. Almon, 1763.
_____, ed. *An Asylum for Fugitive Pieces, in Prose and in Verse, not in any other Collection: with Several Pieces Never before Published.* 4 vols. 1776–79; rpt. London: Printed for J. Debrett, 1785–95.
_____. *Biographical, Literary, and Political Anecdotes of Several of the Most Eminent Persons of the Present Age.* 3 vols. London: T.N. Longman and L.B. Seeley, 1797.
_____. *Books Printed for J. Almon, Opposite Burlington-House, in Piccadilly.* [London: 1775?]
_____. *The Causes of the Present Complaints Fairly Stated and Fully Refuted.* London: Printed for J. Sewell and sold also by W. Owen, J. Downes, and the booksellers of London and Westminister, 1793.

_____, ed. *A Collection of all the Treaties of Peace, Alliance, and Commerce, between Great Britain and Other Powers, from the Revolution in 1688, to the Present Time.* London: Printed for J. Almon, 1772.

_____, ed. *A Collection of Interesting, Authentic Papers, Relative to the Dispute between Great Britain and America; Shewing the Causes and Progress of that Misunderstanding, from 1764 to 1775.* London: Printed for J. Almon, 1777.

_____, ed. *A Collection of Interesting Political Tracts, Published in the Years 1764–1773.* London: J. Almon, 1773.

_____, ed. *A Collection of the Letters of Atticus, Lucius, and Junius.* London: Printed for J. Almon, 1769.

_____, ed. *A Collection of the Most Interesting Tracts, Lately Published in England and America, on the Subjects of Taxing the American Colonies, and Regulating their Trade.* 3 vols. London: Printed for J. Almon, 1766–67.

_____, ed. *A Collection of Tracts, on the Subjects of Taxing the British Colonies in America and Regulating their Trade. In Four Volumes.* London: J. Almon, 1773.

_____, ed. *Companion for a Leisure Hour: Being a Collection of Fugitive Pieces, in Prose and Verse. By Several Gentlemen.* London: Printed for J. Almon, 1769.

_____, ed. *A Complete Collection of the Lord's Protests, from the First upon Record, in the Reign of Henry the Third, to the Present Time.* London: n.p., 1767.

_____. *The Conduct of a Late Noble Commander Examined.* London: S. Fuller, 1759.

_____. *Correspondence of the Late John Wilkes, with his Friends, Printed from the Original Manuscripts, in which are Introduced Memoirs of his Life.* 5 vols. London: Printed for Richard Phillips by Nichols and Son, 1805.

_____, ed. *The Debates and Proceedings of the British House of Commons . . . Compiled from Authentic Papers.* 11 Vols. London: Printed for J. Almon and S. Bladon, 1766–75.

_____. *Free Parliaments: or, a Vindication of the Parliamentary Constitution of England in Answer to Certain Visionary Plans of Modern Reformers.* London: Printed for J. Debrett, 1783.

_____, ed. *The Fugitive Miscellany.* 2 vols. London: J. Almon, 1774–75.

_____, ed. *Fugitive Pieces of Irish Politics, During the Administration of Lord Townshend.* London: Printed for J. Almon, 1772.

_____. *The History of the Late Minority.* 1765; rpt. London: n.p., 1766.

_____. *An History of the Parliament of Great Britain from the Death of Queen Anne to the Death of King George II.* London: Printed for G. Kearsly, 1764.

_____. *An Impartial History of the Late War.* London: Printed for J. Johnson, 1763.

_____, supposed author. *Letters Concerning the Present State of England. Particularly Respecting the Politics, Arts, Manners, and Literature of the Times.* London: J. Almon, 1772.

_____, ed. *The Letters of Junius.* London: Richard Phillips, 1806.

_____. *A Letter to the Earl of Bute.* London: J. Almon, 1767.

_____. *A Letter to J. Kidgell, Containing a Full Answer to his Narrative.* London: J. Williams, 1763.

_____. *A Letter to the Right Honourable Charles Jenkinson.* London: Debrett, 1781.

_____. *A Letter to the Right Hon. George Grenville.* London: J. Williams, 1763.

_____/John Wilkes. *A Letter to the Right Honorable George Grenville, Occasioned by . . . the Speech he Made in the House of Commons on the Motion for Expelling Mr. Wilkes, Friday, February 3, 1769.* London: Printed for Isaac Fell, 1769.

_____. *A List of Books and Pamphlets Printed for J. Almon, opposite Burlington-House, in Piccadilly*. [London: 1769?].

_____, supposed author. *London Courtship*. London: Printed for M. Thrush, [1759?].

_____. *Memoirs of a Late Eminent Bookseller*. London, 1790; facsim. New York: Garland, 1974.

_____. *A New Catalogue of Books and Pamphlets, Printed for J. Almon, Bookseller and Stationer, opposite Burlington-House, Piccadilly*. London, September, 1770. [London: 1770].

_____, ed. *The New Foundling Hospital for Wit*. 6 vols. 1768–73; rpt. London: Debrett, 1786.

_____, ed. *A New and Impartial Collection of Interesting Letters from the Public Papers*. London: Printed for J. Almon, 1767.

_____. *A New Military Dictionary*. London: J. Cooke, 1760.

_____, ed. *Parliamentary Register*. 17 vols. London: J. Almon, 1775–80.

_____. *A Political Paradox*. London: Printed for J. Almon, 1777.

_____, ed. *The Political Register*. London: Printed for J. Almon, 1767.

_____, ed. *The Remembrancer*. London: Printed for J. Almon, 1775–84.

_____. *Review of Lord Bute's Administration*. London: Printed for I. Pridden, 1763.

_____. *Review of Mr. Pitt's Administration*. London: G. Kearsly, 1762.

_____. *Review of the Reign of George the Second*. London: J. Wilkie, 1762.

_____. *The Revolution in MDCCLXXXII Impartially Considered*. London: Debrett, 1782.

_____, ed. *A Select Collection of Interesting Political Tracts*. London: Printed for J. Almon, 1770.

_____, supposed author. *Theatrical Biography: or Memoirs of the Principal Performers of the Three Theatres Royal, Drury Lane, Covent-Garden, Haymarket, with Remarks on their Professional Merits*. 2 vols. London: Printed for S. Bladon, 1772.

_____ and William Beckford. *History of France, from the Most Early Records, to the Death of Louis XVI: The Ancient Part by William Beckford, Esq. . . . the Modern Part by an English Gentleman, who has been Some Time Resident in Paris*. 4 vols. London: J.S. Jordan, 1794.

_____ and Humphrey Cotes. *An Enquiry into the Conduct of a Late Right Honourable Commoner*. London: J. Almon, 1766.

Another Letter to Mr. Almon, in Matter of Libel. London: Printed for J. Almon, 1770.

Balderston, Katharine, ed. *Thraliana: The Diary of Mrs. Hester Lynch Thrale (Later Mrs. Piozzi) 1776–1809*. 2 vols. Oxford: Clarendon Press, 1942.

Bell, John, ed. *Bell's Classical Arrangement of Fugitive Poetry*. 18 vols. London: Printed by J. Bell, 1789–97.

Burke, Edmund. *Substance of the Speeches Made in the House of Commons on Wednesday, the 15th of December, 1779. On Mr. Burke's Giving Notice of his Intention to Bring in a Bill after the Christmas Recess, for the Retrenchment of Public Expences, and for the Better Securing the Independence of Parliament*. London: J. Almon, 1779.

Burke, Edmund, William, and Richard. *The Yorkshire Question*. London: Printed for J. Almon, 1780.

Burke, Richard, with the assistance of William and Edmund Burke. *The Letters of Valens*. London: Printed for J. Almon, 1777.

Burrow, James. *Reports of Cases Argued and Adjudged in the Court of King's Bench*. 5 vols. London: Printed by A. Strahan and W. Woodfall for E. and R. Brooke, 1790.

Cartwright, John. *Take your Choice! Representation and Respect: Imposition and Contempt. Annual Parliaments and Liberty. Long Parliaments and Slavery.* . . . London: Printed for J. Almon, 1776.

"The Ceremony Observed this Day at the Installation of the Duke of Grafton at Cambridge, as Chancellor of that University." *London Chronicle,* 26 (1769), 6–7.

"Chronicle." *Annual Register,* 13 (1770), 115, 121, 165.

Cordasco, Francesco, ed. *The Letters of Tobias George Smollett: A Supplement to the Noyes Collection.* Madrid: Imp. Avelino Ortega, 1950.

Davies, Thomas, ed. *Miscellaneous and Fugitive Pieces.* 3 vols. London: T. Davies, 1773.

Debrett, John. *Catalogue of Books and Pamphlets, Printed and Sold by J. Debrett (successor to Mr. Almon) opposite Burlington House, Piccadilly.* [London: Debrett, 1782].

The Defense of Admiral Keppel. 1779; rpt. London: J. Almon, 1779.

Dickinson, John. *The Late Regulations Respecting the British Colonies on the Continent of America Considered, in a Letter from a Gentleman in Philadelphia to his Friend in London.* 1765; rpt. London: Printed for J. Almon, 1765.

———. *Letters from a Farmer in Pennsylvania to the Inhabitants of the British Colonies.* 1768; rpt. London: J. Almon, 1768.

Dodsley, Robert, ed. *A Collection of Poems . . . by Several Hands.* 6 vols. London: Printed by J. Hughs for R. Dodsley, 1748–58.

———, ed. *Fugitive Pieces on Various Subjects.* 2 vols. 1761; rpt. London: Printed for J. Dodsley, 1771.

Dulany, Daniel. *Considerations on the Propriety of Imposing Taxes in the British Colonies, for the Purpose of Raising a Revenue, by Act of Parliament.* 1765; rpt. London: J. Almon, 1766.

The Examination of Doctor Benjamin Franklin, Relative to the Repeal of the American Stamp Act. 1766; rpt. London: Printed for J. Almon, 1767.

Extracts from the Votes and Proceedings of the American Continental Congress. London: J. Almon, 1775.

"Father of Candor." *An Enquiry into the Doctrine Lately Propagated, Concerning Libels, Warrants, and the Seizure of Papers.* London: Printed for J. Almon, 1764.

The Foundling Hospital for Wit. Intended for the Reception and Preservation of such Brats of Wit and Humour whose Parents Chuse to Drop them. London: Printed for G. Lion, 1743.

Fugitive Pieces. By a Poor Poet. London: Printed for T. Becket and P.A. De Hondt, in the Strand, and C. Etherington at York, 1767.

Fugitive Pieces: A Collection of Original Poems, the Greater Part by the Most Eminent Writers of the Present Age. Edinburgh: Printed for J. Johnson and sold at the Scots Chronicle Office, 1797.

Garrick, David. "Advice to the Marquis of Rockingham." *Annual Register,* 8 (1765), 279.

Gray, Thomas. "Ode to Music, Performed in the Senate House at Cambige [sic], July 1, 1769 at the Installation of Augustus Henry Duke of Grafton, Chancellor of that University." *Gentleman's Magazine,* 39 (1769), 359.

———. "Ode to Music, Performed in the Senate House at Cambridge, July 1, 1769, at the Installation of Augustus Henry Duke of Grafton, Chancellor of the University." *London Chronicle,* 26 (1769), 15–16.

Great Britain, Parliament. House of Commons. [Proceedings.] *The Speech of a Right Honourable Gentleman, on the Motion for Expelling Mr. Wilkes, Friday, February 3, 1769.* London: Printed for J. Almon, 1769.

112

Greene, Jack, ed. *The Nature of Colony Constitutions: Two Pamphlets on the Wilkes Fund Controversy in South Carolina by Sir Egerton Leigh and Arthur Lee.* South Carolina: University of South Carolina Press, 1970.

Guttridge, George H., ed. Vol. III of *The Correspondence of Edmund Burke.* Chicago: University of Chicago Press, 1961.

Headley, Henry. *Fugitive Pieces.* London: Printed for C. Dilly, 1785.

"Historical Chronicle." *Gentleman's Magazine,* 39 (1769), 361.

"Historical Chronicle." *Gentleman's Magazine,* 40 (1770), 541.

Hoffman, Ross, ed. *Edmund Burke, New York Agent with his Letters to the New York Assembly and Intimate Correspondence with Charles O'Hara 1761–1776.* Philadelphia: The American Philosophical Society, 1956.

Hopkins, Stephen. *The Grievances of the American Colonies Candidly Examined.* 1765; rpt. London: J. Almon, 1766.

Howell, Thomas Bayly. *Complete Collection of State Trials.* Ed. Thomas Jones Howell. 34 vols. London: Printed by T.C. Hansard for Longman, Hurst, Rees, Orme, and Brown, etc., 1814–28.

Johnson, Samuel. *A Dictionary of the English Language.* 2 vols. 1755; rpt. London: Printed for J.F. and C. Rivington, L. Davis, etc., 1785.

Knox, William. *Present State of the Nation.* London: Printed for J. Almon, 1768.

Labaree, Leonard, Ralph Ketcham, Helen Boatfield, and Helen Fineman, ed. *The Autobiography of Benjamin Franklin.* 1791; rpt. New Haven: Yale University Press, 1964.

Lee, Arthur. *An Appeal to the Justice and Interests of the People of Great Britain in the Present Dispute with America.* London: J. Almon, 1774.

_____. *Answer to Considerations on Certain Political Transactions of the Province of South Carolina.* London: Printed for J. Almon, 1774.

A Letter to Lord George Germaine, Giving an Account of the Origin of the Dispute between Great Britain and her Colonies. London: Printed for J. Almon, 1776.

A Letter to the Right Honourable Earl of Temple. 1763; rpt. London: S. Bladon, 1766.

A Letter to the Right Honourable Earl Temple upon the Probable Motives and Consequences of his Lordship's Conduct with Regard to Mr. Wilkes. London: Printed for W. Nicoll, 1763.

Lewis, W.S., Grover Cronin, Jr., and Charles Bennett, ed. Vols. XXVIII and XXIX of *Horace Walpole's Correspondence.* New Haven : Yale University Press, 1955.

Lewis, W.S. and Robert A. Smith, ed. Vol. XXX of *Horace Walpole's Correspondence.* New Haven: Yale University Press, 1961.

"List of Books—with Remarks." *Gentleman's Magazine,* 41 (1771), 80–82.

McDowell, R.B. and John Woods, ed. Vol. IX of *The Correspondence of Edmund Burke.* Chicago: University of Chicago Press, 1970.

Mason, William. *The Dean and the 'Squire: A Political Eclogue.* London: Printed for J. Debrett, 1782.

_____. *An Epistle to Dr. Shebbeare: to which is Added an Ode to Sir Fletcher Norton.* London: Printed for J. Almon, 1777.

_____. *An Heroic Epistle to Sir William Chambers.* London: Printed for J. Almon, 1773.

_____. *An Heroic Postscript to the Public, Occasioned by their Favourable Reception of a Late Heroic Epistle to Sir William Chambers. . . .* London: J. Almon, 1774.

_____. *Ode to Mr. Pinchbeck upon his Newly Invented Patent Candle-Snuffers.* London: J. Almon, 1776.

"Mr. Almon." *Public Characters of 1803–1804,* 6 (1804), 120–38.

"Monthly Catalogue." *Monthly Review*, XXV (1762), 502.

"Monthly Catalogue." *Monthly Review*, NS XLVIII (1805), 105.

Monthly Magazine, XV (1803), 151.

The Necessity of Repealing the American Stamp Act Demonstrated. London: Printed for J. Almon, 1766.

Nichols, John. *Literary Anecdotes of the Eighteenth Century*. 9 vols. London: Printed for the author by Nichols, son, and Bentley, 1812–16.

O'Beirne, Thomas. *Candid and Impartial Narrative of the Transactions of the Fleet under the Command of Lord Howe*. London: Printed for J. Almon, 1779.

"Obituary, with Anecdotes of Remarkable Persons." *Gentleman's Magazine*, 75 (1805), 1179–80.

Observations on Several Acts of Parliament . . . by the Merchants of Boston. London: J. Almon, 1770.

Otis, James. *A Vindication of the British Colonies*. 1765; rpt. London: J. Almon, 1769.

Paine, Thomas. *Common Sense*. 1776; rpt. London: J. Almon, 1776.

Parks, Stephen. *The English Book Trade, 1660–1853*. Contemporary sources in facsim. New York: Garland, 1974.

The Parliamentary History of England from the Earliest Period to the Year 1803. London: Printed by T.C. Hansard for Longman, Hurst, Rees, Orme, and Brown, etc., 1806–20.

Potter, Thomas. *An Essay on Woman*. 1763; rpt. London: n.p., 1871.

Pownall, Thomas. *The Right, Interest, and Duty of Government*. 1773; rpt. London: Printed for J. Almon, 1781.

Pratt, Charles (Earl of Camden), supposed author. *Another Letter to Mr. Almon, in Matter of Libel*. London: Printed for J. Almon, 1770.

Reflections on the Case of Mr. Wilkes, and on the Right of the People to Elect their own Representatives. To which is Added the Case of Mr. Walpole. London: Printed for J. Almon, 1768.

A Second Postscript to a Late Pamphlet Entitled A Letter to Mr. Almon. . . . London: J. Miller, 1770.

"A Short Retrospect of the Process against Mr. Almon, Publisher of the Letter on Libels." *Annual Register*, 8 (1765), 177–79.

Smith, William James, ed. *The Grenville Papers*. 4 vols. London: John Murray, 1853.

Sutherland, Lucy, ed. Vol. II of *The Correspondence of Edmund Burke*. Chicago: University of Chicago Press, 1960.

The Trial of John Almon . . . for Selling Junius's Letter to the K---. London: Printed for J. Miller, 1770.

The Trial of John Peter Zenger. . . . To which is now Added . . . the Trial of Mr. William Owen. London: J. Almon, 1765.

Walpole, Horace. *A Counter-Address to the Public, on the Late Dismission of a General Officer*. London: J. Almon, 1764.

———. *Fugitive Pieces in Verse and Prose*. Printed at Strawberry Hill, 1758.

———. *Memoirs of the Reign of King George the Third*. Ed. G.F. Russell Barker. 4 vols. 1822; rpt. New York: G.P. Putnam's Sons, 1894.

Willcox, William B., ed. Vols. XVI and XXI of *The Papers of Benjamin Franklin*. New Haven: Yale University Press, 1978.

Wilkes, John. *The History of England from the Revolution to the Accession of the Brunswick Line*. London: Printed for J. Almon, 1768.

_____. *A Letter to his Grace the Duke of Grafton.* London: Printed for J. Almon, 1767.
_____/John Almon. *A Letter to . . . Grenville.* (See Almon.)
Wilmot, John. *Memoirs of the Life of the Right Honourable Sir John Eardley Wilmot* [by his son]. 1802; rpt. London: J. Nichols and Son, 1811.
Wilmot, John Eardley. *Notes of Opinions and Judgments Delivered in Different Courts by the Right Honourable Sir John Eardley Wilmot.* London: Hansard, 1802.
Woods, John, ed. Vol. IV of *The Correspondence of Edmund Burke.* Chicago: University of Chicago Press, 1963.

Secondary Sources

Adams, Thomas R. *The American Controversy: A Bibliographical Study of the British Pamphlets about the American Disputes, 1764–1783.* New York: Bibliographical Society of America, 1980.
_____. *American Independence the Growth of an Idea: A Bibliographical Study of the American Political Pamphlets Printed between 1764 and 1776 Dealing with the Dispute between Great Britain and her Colonies.* Providence: Brown University Press, 1965.
Aspinall, A. "The Reporting and Publishing of the House of Commons' Debates 1771–1834." In *Essays Presented to Sir Lewis Namier.* Ed. Richard Pares and A.J.P. Taylor. London: Macmillan, 1956, pp. 227–57.
_____. "Statistical Accounts of the London Newspapers in the Eighteenth Century." *The English Historical Review,* 63 (1948), 226.
Belanger, Terry. "A Directory of the London Book Trade, 1766." *Publishing History,* I (1977), 7–48.
Beljame, Alexandre. *Men of Letters and the English Public in the Eighteenth Century.* Trans. E.O. Lorimer. Ed. and intro. Bonamy Dobrée. France, 1881; rpt. London: Kegan Paul, 1948.
Block, Andrew. *The English Novel 1740–1850: A Catalogue Including Prose Romances, Short Stories, and Translations of Foreign Fiction.* 1939; rpt. New York: Oceana Publications, 1962.
Brewer, John. *Party Ideology and Popular Politics at the Accession of George III.* New York: Cambridge University Press, 1976.
Brooke, John. *The Chatham Administration, 1766–1768.* New York: St. Martin's Press, 1956.
Campbell, John. *The Lives of the Chief Justices of England.* 1845–57; rpt. New York: James Cockcroft, 1874.
Case, Arthur. *A Bibliography of English Poetical Miscellanies 1521–1750.* Oxford: Printed for the Bibliographical Society at the University Press, 1936 (for 1929).
Chalmers, Alexander. "Almon (John)." *The General Biographical Dictionary* (1812).
Christie, Ian. *Wilkes, Wyvill, and Reform: The Parliamentary Reform Movement in British Politics 1760–1785.* London: Macmillan, 1962.
Collins, A.S. *Authorship in the Days of Johnson.* 1927; rpt. Clifton, New Jersey: A.M. Kelley, 1973.
Cone, Carl. *Burke and the Nature of Politics.* Lexington: University of Kentucky Press, 1957.
_____. *The English Jacobins: Reformers in Late Eighteenth-Century England.* New York: Scribner's, 1968.

Cordasco, Francesco. *A Junius Bibliography*. 1949; rpt. New York: Burt Franklin, 1974.

Courtney, William Prideaux and David Nichol Smith. *A Bibliography of Samuel Johnson*. 1915; rpt. Oxford: Clarendon Press, 1968.

Draper, John. *William Mason: A Study in Eighteenth-Century Culture*. New York: New York University Press, 1924.

The Eighteenth-Century Short Title Catalogue.

Foss, Michael. *The Age of Patronage*. Ithaca: Cornell University Press, 1972.

Fox, John. "*The King* v. *John Almon*." *The Law Quarterly Review*, XXIV (1908), 184–98 and 266–78.

_____. "The Summary Process to Punish Contempt." *The Law Quarterly Review*, XXV (1909), 238–54 and 354–71.

Foxon, David. *English Verse 1701–1750: A Catalogue of Separately Printed Poems with Notes on Contemporary Collected Editions*. 2 vols. New York: Cambridge University Press, 1975.

George, Mary Dorothy. Vol V of *Catalogue of Political and Personal Satires Preserved in the Department of Prints and Drawings in the British Museum*. London: Kegan Paul, 1935.

Goldgar, Bertrand. *Walpole and the Wits*. Lincoln: University of Nebraska Press, 1976.

Greene, Donald. "A Reply." *Johnsonian News Letter*, XLIII (1983), 7–8.

Greene, Kenneth. "Sir Robert Walpole and Literary Patronage." Diss. Columbia University 1964.

Gronbeck, Bruce. "Almon, John." *Biographical Dictionary of Modern British Radicals* (1979).

Haig, Robert. *The Gazetteer 1735–1797*. Carbondale: Southern Illinois University Press, 1960.

Halkett, Samuel and John Laing. *Dictionary of Anonymous and Pseudonymous English Literature*. Edinburgh: Oliver and Boyd, 1926.

Halsband, Robert. "Literary Patronage in Eighteenth-Century England" [abstract only]. In *Expression, Communication and Experience in Literature and Language*. Ed. Ronald Popperwell. Proc of the XII Congress of the International Federation for Modern Languages and Literatures, 20–26 August 1972. Leeds: Modern Humanities Research Association, 1973, pp. 186–87.

Hanson, Laurence. *Government and the Press, 1695–1763*. London: Oxford University Press, 1936.

Hart, W.H. "Letters of Junius." *Notes and Queries*, 3rd ser., VIII (1865), 230–33.

Hazen, Allen. *A Bibliography of Horace Walpole*. New Haven: Yale University Press, 1948.

_____. *A Bibliography of the Strawberry Hill Press*. New Haven: Yale University Press, 1942.

Hessler, Mabel. "The Literary Opposition to Sir Robert Walpole." Diss. University of Chicago 1934.

Knapp, Lewis Mansfield. "Forged 'Smollett' Letters." *Notes and Queries*, 198 (1953), 163.

_____. *Tobias Smollett, Doctor of Men and Manners*. Princeton: Princeton University Press, 1949.

Korshin, Paul. Rev. of *The Age of Patronage* by Michael Foss. *Eighteenth-Century Studies*, 7 (1973), 102.

_____. "Types of Eighteenth-Century Literary Patronage." *Eighteenth-Century Studies*, 7 (1974), 453–73.

Langford, P. *The First Rockingham Administration: 1765–1766*. London: Oxford University Press, 1973.

Laurenson, Diana and Alan Swingewood. *The Sociology of Literature*. London: Mac-Gibbon and Kee, 1972.

Lutnick, Solomon. *The American Revolution and the British Press 1775–1783*. Missouri: University of Missouri Press, 1967.

McCoy, Ralph. *Freedom of the Press: An Annotated Bibliography*. Carbondale: Southern Illinois University Press, 1968.

_____. *Freedom of the Press, A Bibliocyclopedia: Ten-Year Supplement (1967–1977)*. Carbondale: Southern Illinois University Press, 1979.

McCracken, David. *Junius and Philip Francis*. Boston: Twayne, 1979.

Maxted, Ian. *The London Book Trades 1775–1800*. Kent: Dawson, 1977.

Nebenzahl, Kenneth. *A Bibliography of Printed Battle Plans of the American Revolution 1775–1795*. Chicago: University of Chicago Press, 1975.

Nobbe, George. *The North Briton: A Study in Political Propaganda*. New York: Columbia University Press, 1939.

Plomer, H.R., G.H. Bushnell, and E.R. Dix. *A Dictionary of Printers and Booksellers who were at Work in England Scotland and Ireland from 1726 to 1775*. London: Printed for the Bibliographical Society at Oxford University Press, 1932 (for 1930).

Postgate, Raymond. *That Devil Wilkes*. New York: Vanguard Press, 1929.

Potts, Lewis W. *Arthur Lee: A Virtuous Revolutionary*. Baton Rouge: Louisiana State University Press, 1981.

Rea, Robert. "Amelia Evans Barry and Gov. Pownall's Map." *Indiana Quarterly for Bookmen*, V (1949), 7–17.

_____. "Bookseller as Historian." *The Indiana Quarterly for Bookmen*, V (1949), 75–95.

_____. *The English Press in Politics 1760–1774*. Lincoln: University of Nebraska Press, 1963.

_____. "John Almon: Bookseller to John Wilkes." *The Indiana Quarterly for Bookmen*, IV (1948), 20–28.

_____. "Mason, Walpole, and that Rogue Almon." *Huntington Library Quarterly*, XXIII (1960), 187–93.

Rogers, Deborah. "Newer Light on Johnson." *Johnsonian News Letter*, XLIII (1983), 13–14.

_____. "The Whittlewood Controversy." *Notes and Queries*, NS 31 (1984), 407.

Rudé, George. *Hanoverian London 1714–1808*. Los Angeles: University of California Press, 1971.

_____. *Wilkes and Liberty: A Social Study of 1763 to 1774*. Oxford: Clarendon Press, 1962.

Ryskamp, Charles and John Baird, ed. Vol. I of *The Poems of William Cowper*. New York: Oxford University Press, 1980.

Sabin, Joseph and Wilberforce Eames. *Bibliotheca America: A Dictionary of Books Relating to America, from its Discovery to the Present Time*. New York: Printed for the Bibliographical Society of America, 1868–1936.

Siebert, Frederick. *Freedom of the Press in England, 1476–1776: The Rise and Decline of Government Controls*. Urbana: University of Illinois Press, 1952.

Smith, D. Nichol. "The Newspaper." in *Johnson's England: An Account of the Life and Manners of his Age*. Ed. A.S. Turberville. 1933; rpt. Oxford: Clarendon Press, 1952, II, 331–67.

Smith, Edward. "Almon, John." *Dictionary of National Biography* (1885).

Straus, Ralph. *Robert Dodsley, Poet, Publisher and Playwright*. New York: John Lane, 1910.

117

Sutherland, James. *A Preface to Eighteenth-Century Poetry*. 1948; rpt. Oxford: Clarendon Press, 1958.

Thomas, Peter D.G. "The Beginning of Parliamentary Reporting in Newspapers, 1768–1774." *The English Historical Review*, LXXIV (1959), 623–36.

_____. "John Wilkes and the Freedom of the Press (1771)." *Bulletin of the Institute of Historical Research*, XXXIII (1960), 86–98.

Timperley, C.H. *Encyclopedia of Literary and Typographical Anecdote*. Introd. Terry Belanger. 2 vols. 1839; 1842 edn. in facsim. New York: Garland, 1977.

Todd, William. *A Bibliography of Edmund Burke*. London: Hart-Davis, 1964.

_____. *A Directory of Printers and Others in Allied Trades, London and Vicinity 1800–1840*. London: Printing Historical Society, 1972.

Valentine, Alan. "Almon, John." *The British Establishment, 1760–1784* (1970).

_____. *Lord George Germain*. Oxford: The Clarendon Press, 1962.

Wallis, N. Hardy. "*Fugitive Poetry*: An Eighteenth-Century Collection." *Essays by Divers Hands: Being the Transactions of the Royal Society of Literature of the United Kingdom*, NS XVIII (1940), 43–66.

Watson, D.H. "The Rise of the Opposition at Wildman's." *Bulletin of the Institute of Historical Research*, XLIV (1971), 57–77.

Watson, George. *The New Cambridge Bibliography of English Literature*. Cambridge: The University Press, 1971.

Watt, Ian. *The Rise of the Novel*. 1957; rpt. Berkeley: University of California Press, 1967.

Watt, Robert. "Almon, John." *Bibliotheca Britannica* (1824).

Werkmeister, Lucyle. *The London Daily Press, 1772–1797*. Lincoln: University of Nebraska Press, 1963.

Williams, Iolo. *Seven Eighteenth-Century Bibliographies*. 1924; rpt. New York: Burt Franklin, 1968.

Williamson, Audrey. *Wilkes: A Friend to Liberty*. New York: E.P. Dutton, 1974.

Wing, Donald. *Short-Title Catalogue of Books Printed in England, Scotland, Ireland, Wales, and British America, and of English Books Printed in Other Countries, 1641–1700*. New York: The Index Society, 1945–51.

Woodfall, Robert. "Before Hansard." *History Today*, 23 (1973), 195–202.

Appendix

Works Issued under Almon's Imprint

This list is based on an examination of trade catalogues, Opposition pamphlets, works by Almon's acquaintances, and references in contemporary memoirs, diaries, and correspondence. Other materials for this investigation included reviews, notices, and advertisements, particularly in magazines and newspapers that Almon had a concern in, such as the *Gazetteer*, the *London Evening Post*, the *Remembrancer*, and the *General Advertiser*. Advertisements in books printed for Almon and for his successor, Debrett, also served as useful guides. Of more significant value, of course, were Almon's own works, papers, and catalogues. General references that were consulted include Halkett and Laing, Sabin, Adams, Evans, Watt, Lowndes, and Allibone, as well as the NUC, the BMC, and the British Museum *Catalogue of Political and Personal Satires*. The computer-based Almon file of the ESTC was invaluable, even though it is often inaccurate and incomplete. While the present study attempts to provide the most exhaustive list of Almon's publications that can be assembled to date, it should be noted that since the ESTC is an ongoing project, it is entirely possible that more works associated with Almon will be discovered.

In what follows, all errors from references cited above have been silently corrected. Entries are arranged alphabetically in the interest both of registering different editions with as much brevity as possible and of emphasizing Almon's network of connections. Unless otherwise indicated, the imprint of successive editions is the same as that of the first edition. Capitalization and punctuation have been modernized, and variations in titles are not recorded.

An Account of Denmark, Ancient and Modern. London: Printed for J. Almon, 1768.

Acherley, Roger. *Reasons for Uniformity in the State.* London: Printed for John Bew and sold by J. Almon and H. Payne, 1780.

Adair, James. *Observations on the Power of Alienation in the Crown before the First of Queen Anne. . . . Together with some Remarks on the Conduct of Administration Respecting the Case of the Duke of Portland.* London: Printed for J. Almon, 1768.

————. *Thoughts on the Dismission of Officers, Civil or Military for their Conduct in Parliament.* London: Printed for J. Almon, 1765.

Addington, William. *An Abridgment of Penal Statutes. . . .* London: Printed by W. Strahan and M. Woodfall for the author and sold by Almon [and at least nine others], [1778?].

Additions to Common Sense: Addressed to the Inhabitants of America. Philadelphia; rpt. London: J. Almon, 1776.

An Address to the Freeholders of Middlesex. London: Printed for J. Almon [and four others], [1780?].

An Address to the Lords of the Admiralty, on their Conduct towards Admiral Keppel. London: Printed for J. Almon, 1778.

An Address to the People of England; Shewing the Advantages Arising from the Frequent Changes of Ministers. . . . London: Printed for the author and sold by J. Almon, 1766.

An Address to the Representatives in Parliament upon the State of the Nation. London: Printed for J. Almon, 1779.

An Address to the Right Honourable L-d M-sf-d; in which the Measures of Government, Respecting America, are Considered in a New Light. . . . London: Printed for J. Almon, 1775.

The Adventure of a Bale of Goods from America, in Consequence of the Stamp Act. London: Printed for J. Almon, 1766.

Alderson, Richard. *The True Alarm.* London: Printed for the author and sold by J. Almon, 1770.

Alleyne, John. *The Legal Degrees of Marriage Stated and Considered in a Series of Letters to a Friend.* London: Printed for J. Almon [and five others], 1775.

"The Allies." Engraving. London: J. Almon, 1780.

Almon, John. *An Appendix to the Review of Mr. Pitt's Administration.* London: J. Almon, 1763.

————, ed. *An Asylum for Fugitives.* Vol. 1. London: Printed for J. Almon, 1776.
Another edition in two volumes, 1776–79.
Another edition printed for J. Debrett, 1785.
Another edition, 4 vols., 1785–95.
Another edition, 4 vols., 1785–99.
Another edition, 4 vols., 1793.
Another edition, 4 vols., 1799.

————. *Books Printed for J. Almon, Opposite Burlington-House in Piccadilly.* [London: J. Almon, 1775?].

_____, ed. *A Collection of all the Treaties of Peace, Alliance, and Commerce, between Great Britain and Other Powers, from the Revolution in 1688, to the Present Time.* London: Printed for J. Almon, 1772.

_____, ed. *A Collection of Interesting, Authentic Papers, Relative to the Dispute between Great Britain and America.* London: Printed for J. Almon, 1777.

_____, ed. *A Collection of Interesting Political Tracts, Published in the Years 1764–1773.* London: J. Almon, 1773.

_____, ed. *A Collection of the Letters of Atticus, Lucius, and Junius.* London: Printed for J. Almon, 1769.

Two more editions, 1769.

_____, ed. *A Collection of the Most Interesting Tracts, Lately Published in England and America.* 3 vols. London: Printed for J. Almon, 1766–67.

_____, ed. *A Collection of Tracts, on the Subjects of Taxing the British Colonies in America and Regulating their Trade.* 4 vols. London: J. Almon, 1773.

_____, ed. *Companion for a Leisure Hour.* London: Printed for J. Almon, 1769.

_____, ed. *The Debates and Proceedings of the British House of Commons.* 11 vols. London: Printed for J. Almon and S. Bladon, 1766–75.

_____, ed. *The Fugitive Miscellany.* 2 vols. London: J. Almon, 1774–75.

_____, ed. *Fugitive of Pieces of Irish Politics, During the Administration of Lord Townshend.* London: Printed for J. Almon, 1772.

_____, supposed author. *Letters Concerning the Present State of England.* London: J. Almon, 1772.

_____. *A Letter to the Earl of Bute.* London: J. Almon, 1767.

_____. *A List of Books and Pamphlets Printed for J. Almon.* [London: J. Almon, 1769?].

_____. *A New Catalogue of Books and Pamphlets Printed for J. Almon.* [London: J. Almon, 1770].

_____, ed. *The New Foundling Hospital for Wit.* 6 vols. London: Printed for J. Almon, 1768. [First issued as a periodical.]

Part 1, third edition, 1771.

Part 4, 1771.

Part 6, 1773.

Third edition, 6 vols., 1769–76.

A new edition, 6 vols. London: Printed for J. Debrett, 1784.

Another edition, 6 vols., 1786.

Another edition, 1796.

_____, ed. [*A Collection of the Most Interesting Political Letters*] *A New and Impartial Collection of Interesting Letters from the Public Papers.* 2 vols. London: Printed for J. Almon, 1767.

_____, ed. *Parliamentary Register.* 17 vols. London: J. Almon, 1775–1780. [See Great Britain.]

_____. *A Political Paradox.* London: Printed for J. Almon, 1777.

_____, ed. *The Political Register.* London: Printed for J. Almon, 1767.

_____, ed. *The Remembrancer.* 17 vols. London: Printed for J. Almon, 1775–84.

_____, ed. *A Select Collection of Interesting Political Tracts.* London: Printed for J. Almon, 1770.

_____ and Humphrey Cotes. *An Enquiry into the Conduct of a Late Right Honourable Commoner.* London: J. Almon, 1766.

Four more editions, 1766.

America, an Ode. To the People of England. London: Printed for J. Almon, 1776.

Anstey, Christopher. *Appendix to The Patriot.* London: Sold by J. Almon [and three others].

———. *A Familiar Epistle from C. Anstey, Esq. to C.W. Bampfylde, Esq.* London: Printed for J. Almon, 1777.

Second edition, 1777.

———. *The New Bath Guide.* London: Sold by J. Almon [among others], 1766.

Second and third editions, 1766.

———. *The Patriot.* London: Sold by J. Almon [among others], 1767.

Second edition, 1768.

Answer to Considerations on Certain Political Transactions of the Province of South Carolina. London: Printed for J. Almon, 1774.

An Answer to a Pamphlet Entitled Taxation No Tyranny. London: Printed for J. Almon, 1775.

An Answer to a Pamphlet Written by Doctor Lettsom Entitled Observations Preparatory to the use of Dr. Mayersbach's Medicines. London: Printed for J. Almon, 1776.

Author of the E-1 of Ch-m's Apology. *An Ode to the Earl of Ch-m.* London: Printed for J. Almon, 1767.

Author of the Essay on the Rights of the East-India Company. *Considerations on the Important Benefits to be Derived from the East-India Company's Building and Navigating their own Ships.* London: Printed for J. Almon, 1778.

An Authentic Account of the Part Taken by the Late Earl of Chatham in a Transaction which Passed in the Beginning of the Year 1778. London: Printed for J. Almon, 1778.

Second and third editions, 1778.

Authentic Account of the Proceedings of the Congress Held at New-York, in MDCCLXV, on the Subject of the American Stamp Act. [London: Printed for J. Almon?], 1767.

Baillie, Thomas, Captain. *A Solemn Appeal to the Public, from an Injured Officer, Captain Baillie, Late Lieutenant Governor, of the Royal Hospital for Seamen at Greenwich; Arising out of a Series of Authentic Proceedings in the Court of King's-Bench on Six Prosecutions against him, for Publishing Certain Libels. . . .* London: Printed for Captain Baillie by J. Almon; and may also be had of Captain Baillie, at Mr. Roberts, 1779.

"The Balance of Credit." Engraving. London: J. Almon, 1772.

Baynes, John. *Ode Occasioned by Sir William Browne's Legacy of Two Gold Medals, to be Disposed of Annually, for the Encouragement of Poetry in the University of Cambridge.* London: Printed for J. Almon, 1776.

The Begining [sic], Progress, and Conclusion of the Late War, with Other Interesting Matters Considered; and a Map of the Lands, Islands, Gulphs, Seas, and Fishing-Banks, Comprising the Cod Fishery in America. . . . London: Printed for J. Almon, 1770.

Bentinck, William Henry Cavendish, Duke of Portland (3rd). *The Case of his Grace the Duke of Portland, Respecting Two Leases Lately Granted by the Lords of the Treasury to Sir James Lowther, Bart. with Observations on the Motion for a Remedial Bill, for Quieting the Possession of the Subject.* London: Printed for J. Almon, 1768.

Ten more editions, 1768.

Bengal, Governor and Council. *Authentic Abstracts of Minutes in the Supreme Council of Bengal on the Late Contracts for Draught and Carriage Bullocks, for Victualling the European Troops. . . .* London: Printed for J. Almon, 1780.

———. *Proceedings of the Governor and Council at Fort William, Respecting the Administration of Justice amongst the Natives in Bengal.* London: Printed for J. Almon, 1775.

122

Bernard, Sir Francis, Bart. *Letters to the Right Honourable the Earl of Hillsborough, from Governor Bernard, General Gage, and the Honourable His Majesty's Council for the Province of Massachusetts-Bay.* . . . Boston, 1769; rpt. London: John Almon, [1769].

Bertie, Willoughby, Earl of Abingdon (4th). *Dedication to the Collective Body of the People of England, in which the Source of our Present Political Distractions are [sic] Pointed out, and a Plan Proposed for their Remedy and Redress.* Oxford: Printed for W. Jackson and sold by J. Almon, J. Bew, J. Ridley, R. Faulder, and H. Payne, London; and by the booksellers of Bristol and Bath, 1780.

———. *Thoughts on the Letter of Edmund Burke, Esq. to the Sheriffs of Bristol, on the Affairs of America.* Oxford: Printed for W. Jackson and sold by J. Almon and J. Bew, London; and by the booksellers of Bristol, Bath, and Cambridge, [1777].
Five more editions, 1777.
Seventh edition, 1780.

Blanchard, William Isaac. *A Complete System of Short Hand, being an Improvement upon all the Authors whose Systems have yet been Made Public; is Easy to be Attained, and may be Read Again at any Distance of Time with the Greatest Certainty.* . . . London: Printed for the author and sold by him; also by J. Almon [and three others], 1779.

Bland, Richard. *An Enquiry into the Rights of the British Colonies; Intended as an Answer to "The Regulations Lately Made Concerning the Colonies, and the Taxes Imposed upon them Considered".* [London, Williamsburg; rpt. London: J. Almon, 1769].

Bollan, William. *Continued Corruption, Standing Armies, and Popular Discontents Considered; and the Establishment of the English Colonies in America.* . . . London: Printed and sold by J. Almon, 1768.

———. *An Essay on the Right of Every Man in a Free State to Speak and Write Freely in Order to Defend the Public Rights and Promote the Public Welfare; and on Various Great Occasions for the Present Use of it.* London: Printed and sold by J. Almon, 1772.

———. *The Petitions of Mr. Bollan, Agent for the Council of the Province of Massachusetts Bay, Lately Presented to the Two Houses of Parliament.* . . . London: Printed and sold by J. Almon, 1774.

———. *The Petition of Mr. Bollan, Agent for the Council of the Province of Massachusetts Bay, to the King in Council, Dated January 26, 1774. Published . . . to Shew to the Impartial and Considerate the Importance of Perfect Harmony between Great Britain and the Colonies.* . . . London: Printed and sold by J Almon, 1774.

———. *The Rights of the English Colonies Established in America Stated and Defended; their Merits and Importance to Great Britain Displayed; with Illustration of the Benefits of their Union, and of the Mischiefs and Dangers of their Continued Dissention.* London: Printed and sold by J. Almon, 1774.

Bolts, William. *Considerations on India Affairs; Particularly Respecting the Present State of Bengal and its Dependencies.* . . . London: Printed for J. Almon, P. Elmsly, and Brotherton and Sewell, 1772.
Two more editions, 1772–1775.

Bonesana, Cesare, Marchese di Beccaria. *An Essay on Crimes and Punishments, Translated from the Italian; with a Commentary, Attributed to Mons. de Voltaire, Translated from the French.* London: Printed for J. Almon, 1767.

Boston, Mass. *An Appeal to the World; or a Vindication of the Town of Boston from Many False and Malicious Aspersions Contained in Certain Letters and Memorials, Written by*

Governor Bernard, General Gage, Commodore Hood, the Commissioners of the American Board of Customs, and Others. . . . Boston: Printed by Edes and Gill; rpt. London: J. Almon, 1770.

Boswell, George, of Piddletown. *A Treatise on Watering Meadows. Wherein are Shewn Some of the Many Advantages Arising from that Mode of Practice, Particularly on Coarse, Boggy, or Barren Lands. . . .* London: Printed for the author and sold by J. Almon, 1779.

"Britain's State Pilot Foundering on Taxation Rock." London: J. Almon, 1779.

Brownsmith, John. *The Dramatic Time-Piece: or Perpetual Monitor.* London: Printed for J. Almon, T. Davis, and J. Hingeston, 1767.

Burgoyne, Right Hon. John. *A Letter from Lieut. Gen. Burgoyne to his Constituents upon his Late Resignation; with the Correspondences between the Secretaries of War and him, Relative to his Return to America.* London: Printed for J. Almon, 1779.
Five more editions, 1779.

_____. *A State of the Expedition from Canada, as Laid before the House of Commons, by Lieutenant-General Burgoyne . . . with a Collection of Authentic Documents . . . Written and Collected by himself. . . .* London: Printed for J. Almon, 1780.
Second edition, 1780.

_____. *The Substance of General Burgoyne's Speeches on Mr. Vyner's Motion on the 26th of May and upon Mr. Hartley's Motion on the 28th of May, 1778. With an Appendix Containing General Washington's Letter to General Burgoyne.* London: Printed for J. Almon, 1778.
Second and third editions, 1778.

Burke, Edmund. *Substance of the Speeches Made in the House of Commons on Wednesday the 15th of December, 1779.* London: J. Almon, 1779.

Burke, Edmund (with John Christopher Roberts/William Mellish?). *A True History of a Late Short Administration.* 1766; rpt. London: J. Almon, 1766.

Burke, Richard, Edmund, and William. *The Letters of Valens (which originally appeared in the London Evening Post) with Corrections, Explanatory Notes, and a Preface, by the Author.* London: Printed by J. Almon, 1777.

_____. *The Yorkshire Question.* London: Printed for J. Almon, [1780].

Burrows, John, M.D. *A New Practical Essay on Cancers. . . . To which is also Added a New, More Safe, and Efficacious Method of Administering Hemlock.* London: Printed for the author and sold by W. Owen and J. Almon, 1767.

Butler, John, Bishop of Hereford. *Some Account of the Character of the Late Right Honourable Henry Bilson Legge.* London: Printed for J. Almon, 1764.
Second and third editions, 1765.

C.W. *The Honest Elector's Proposal for Rendering the Votes of all Constituents throughout the Kingdom Free and Independent.* London: Printed for the author and sold by J. Almon, 1767.

A Candid Enquiry into the Present Ruined State of the French Monarchy. With Remarks on the Late Despotick Reduction of the Interest of the National Debt of France. London: Printed for J. Almon, 1770.

Candor. *A Letter to the Public Advertiser.* London: Printed for J. Almon, 1764.
Second edition, 1764.
Third edition, 1770.

Canning, George. *An Appeal to the Publick from the Malicious Misrepresentations, Impudent Falsifications, and Unjust Decisions of the Anonymous Fabricators of the Critical Review.* London: Sold by J. Dodsley, J. Almon, T. Becket, and W. Flexney, 1767.

———. *A Letter to the Right Honourable Wills Earl of Hillsborough on the Connection between Great Britain and her American Colonies.* London: Printed for T. Becket and J. Almon, 1768.

———. *Poems.* London: Printed for the author and sold by J. Almon [and 8 others], 1767.

Caron de Beaumarchais, Pierre Augustin. *Observations sur le memoire justificatif de la cour de Londres.* Londres: Chez J. Almon, 1780.

Cartwright, John, Major. *A Letter to the Earl of Abingdon Discussing a Position Relative to a Fundamental Right of the Constitution. . . .* London: Printed for J. Almon, 1778.

———. *The People's Barrier against Undue Influence and Corruption or the Commons' House of Parliament According to the Constitution. . . .* London: Printed for J. Almon, 1780. Second edition, 1780.

———. *Take your Choice! Representation and Respect: Imposition and Contempt. Annual Parliaments and Liberty: Long Parliaments and Slavery.* London: Printed for J. Almon, 1776. Second edition, 1777.

Cary, George Saville. *Momus, a Poem; or a Critical Examination into the Merits of the Performers and Comic Pieces at the Theatre-Royal in the Hay-Market.* London: Printed for the author and sold by J. Almon and J. Williams, [1767].

The Case of the President or Governor and of the Council of Madrass. . . . London: Printed for J. Almon, 1777.

Cato. *An Essay on the English Constitution.* London: Printed for the author and sold by J. Almon, 1770.

A Caveat on the Part of Public Credit, Previous to the Opening of the Budget, for the Present Year, 1768. London: Printed for J. Almon, 1768. Second edition, 1768.

Chalmers, James. *Plain Truth: Addressed to the Inhabitants of America. Containing Remarks on a Late Pamphlet Intitled Common Sense. . . .* London and Philadelphia; rpt. London: J. Almon, 1776. Second edition, 1776.

The Charters of the British Colonies in America. London: Printed for J. Almon, [1775?]. Second edition, 1775(?)

The Charters of the Following Provinces of North America; viz. Virginia, Maryland, Connecticut, Rhode Island, Pensylvania [sic], Massachusett's Bay, and Georgia. To which is Prefixed a Faithful Narrative of the Proceedings of the North American Colonies in Consequence of the Late Stamp-Act. London: Printed for W. Owen, J. Almon, and F. Blyth, 1766. Two more editions, 1766.

Churchill, Charles. *The Author.* London: J. Almon [and 5 others], 1763. Second edition, 1764.

———. *The Candidate.* London: Printed for the author and sold by J. Almon [and 6 others], 1764.

———. *The Conference.* London: J. Almon [and 5 others], 1763. Two more editions, 1764.

———. *The Duellist.* London: J. Almon [and 5 others], 1764. Two more editions, 1764.

————. *The Farewell*. London: Printed for the author and sold by J. Almon [and 6 others], 1764.

————. *The Ghost. Book IV*. London: Printed for J. Almon [and 5 others], 1763.

————. *Gotham. A Poem. Book I*. London: Printed for the author and sold by J. Almon [and 5 others], 1764.

————. *Gotham. A Poem. Book II*. London: Printed for the author and sold by J. Almon [and 5 others], 1764.

————. *Gotham. A Poem. Book III*. London: Printed for the author and sold by J. Almon [and 5 others], 1764.

————. *Independence*. London: Printed for the author and sold by J. Almon [and 5 others], 1764.

————. *Poems*. London: Printed for the author by Dryden Leach and sold by J. Almon [and 7 others], 1763.

————. *The Times*. Printed for the author and sold by J. Almon [and 5 others], 1764.

Cluny, Alexander. *The American Traveller or Observations on the Present State, Culture and Commerce of the British Colonies in America*. . . . London: Printed for E. and C. Dilly and J. Almon, 1769.

A Companion to the Royal Kalendar . . . to November, 1773. London: Printed for J. Almon, 1774.

A Companion to the Royal Kalendar . . . to the End of October, 1774. . . . *The fourth edition*. London: Printed for J. Almon, 1775.

A Companion to the Royal Kalendar for the year 1776. . . . *The Ninth Edition, Corrected*. London: Printed for J. Almon, 1776.

A Companion to the Royal Kalendar, for the Year 1777. . . . *The Thirteenth Edition. Corrected to the 15th of November, 1776*. London: Printed for J. Almon, 1776.

A Companion to the Royal Kalendar, for the Year 1777. . . . *The Fifteenth edition*. London: Printed for J. Almon, 1777.

A Companion to the Royal Kalendar, for the Year 1779. . . . *The Twenty Fourth Edition. With a Complete Index of all Names*. London: Printed for J. Almon, 1779.

A Companion to the Royal Kalendar for the Year 1781. . . . *The Twenty Eighth Edition. With an Appendix*. London: Printed for J. Almon, 1780.

A Companion to the Royal Kalendar for the Year 1781. . . . *The Twenty Ninth Edition. With an Appendix*. London: Printed for J. Almon and J. Debrett, 1781.

Considerations on the Dearness of Corn and Provisions. . . . London: Printed for J. Almon, 1767.

Considerations on the Imposition of 41/2 Per Cent. Collected on Grenada and the Southern Charibbee Islands . . . without Grant of Parliament. London: Printed for J. Almon, 1774.

Considerations on the Policy, Commerce and Circumstances of the Kingdom. London: Printed for J. Almon, 1771.

Considerations on the Times. London: Printed for J. Almon, 1769.

A Constitutional Answer to the Rev. Mr. John Wesley's Calm Address to the American Colonies. London: Printed for E. and C. Dilly and J. Almon, 1775.

Constitutionalis's Letters to the Electors and People of England Preparatory to the Approaching General Election. London: Printed for J. Almon and W. Flexney, 1780.

The Contest. A Poem. London: Printed for J. Almon, 1764.

Continental Congress. *Journal of the Proceedings of the Congress Held at Philadelphia, May 10, 1775*. London and Philadelphia; rpt. London: J. Almon, 1776.

Cook, James. *A Second Voyage Round the World.* . . . London: Printed for the editor and sold by J. Almon [among others], 1776.
Country Gentleman. *The Advantages and Disadvantages of Inclosing Waste Lands and Open Fields, Impartially Stated and Considered.* London: Printed for J. Almon, 1772.
————. *The Complete Grazier or Gentleman and Farmer's Directory. Containing the Best Instructions for Buying, Breeding and Feeding Cattle, Sheep and Hogs, and for Suckling Lambs.* London: Printed for J. Almon, 1767.
Second edition, 1767.
Third edition,?
Fourth edition, 1776.
————. *Four Letters from the Country Gentleman on the Subject of the Petitions.* London: Printed for J. Almon, 1780.
————. *A Parallel Drawn between the Administration in the Last Four Years of Queen Anne and the Four First of George the Third.* London: Printed for J. Almon, 1766.
The Crisis: Being Three State Poems on the Following Subjects: I. The Northern Dictator. . . . *II. On the Reduction and Surrender of the Havannah.* . . . *III. Caledonia.* . . . London: Printed for J. Williams and J. Almon, 1764.
Cunningham, John. *Poems, Chiefly Pastoral.* London: Printed for the author and sold by J. Almon [and 7 others], 1766.
Dalrymple, John, Earl of Stair (5th). *Considerations Preliminary to the Fixing the Supplies, the Ways and Means, and the Taxes for the Year 1781.* . . . London: Printed for J. Almon and J. Debrett, 1781.
————. *The State of the National Debt, the National Income, and the National Expenditure. With Some Short Inferences and Reflections Applicable to the Present Dangerous Crisis.* London: Printed for J. Almon, 1776.
Three more editions, 1776.
Dalrymple, William, Lieutenant-Colonel. *Travels through Spain and Portugal in 1774 with a Short Account of the Spanish Expedition against Algiers in 1775.* London: Printed for J. Almon, 1777.
The Danger and Immodesty of the Present too General Custom of Unnecessarily Employing Men-Midwives. Proved Incontestibly in the Letters which Lately Appeared under the Signature of a Man-Midwife. With an Introduction, a Treatise on the Milk, and an Appendix. London: Printed for J. Almon [and 3 others], 1772.
Second edition, 1772.
Day, Thomas. *Ode for the New Year, 1776.* London: Printed for J. Almon, 1776.
The Defence of Admiral Keppel. 1779; rpt. London: J. Almon, 1779. (Published simultaneously with *The Proceedings at Large.* . . .)
A Defence of Some Proceedings Lately Depending in Parliament, to Render More Effectual the Act for Quieting the Possession of the Subject, Commonly Called the Nullum Tempus Act. London: Printed for J. Almon, 1771.
The Description of a Parliament in no Instance Similar to the Present. London: Printed for J. Almon, 1769.
Detester of Jobs under All Administrations. *Short Considerations upon Some Late Extraordinary Grants. And Other Particulars of a Late Patriot's Conduct.* London: J. Almon, 1766.
Dickinson, John. *The Late Regulations Respecting the British Colonies on the Continent of America Considered, in a Letter from a Gentleman in Philadelphia to his Friend in London.*

Philadelphia, 1765; rpt. London: J. Almon, 1765 [1766?].
Second edition, 1765 [1766?].
Third edition, 1766.

————. *Letters from a Farmer in Pennsylvania to the Inhabitants of the British Colonies.* Boston, 1768; rpt. London: J. Almon, 1768.
Another edition, 1774.

————. *A New Essay by the Pennsylvanian Farmer on the Constitutional Power of Great-Britain over the Colonies in America with the Resolves of the Committee for the Province of Pennsylvania.* . . . Philadelphia; rpt. London: J. Almon, 1774.

Dicks, John. *The New Gardener's Dictionary or Whole Art of Gardening.* . . . London: Printed for J. Almon [and 4 others], 1771.

Dominiceti, Bartholomew de. *Medical Anecdotes of the Last Thirty Years.* . . . London: Printed for Mess. Almon and Debrett [and 4 others], 1781.

Donellan, John. *The Proceedings at Large on the Trial of John Donellan, Esq. for the Wilful Murder (by Poison) of Sir The. Edward Allesley Broughton.* . . . London: Printed for J. Almon and J. Debrett [and at least 5 others], [1781].

Downing, George. *The Volunteers . . . A Comedy of One Act.* . . . London: Printed for J. Almon, G. Kearsley and J. Wilkie, 1780.

Doyle, William. *Some Account of the British Dominions beyond the Atlantic.* . . . London: Printed for the author by J. Browne and sold by J. Almon [and 6 others], [1770?].

Dragonetti, Giacinto, Marchese. *A Treatise on Virtues and Rewards.* London: Printed for Johnson and Payne and J. Almon, 1769.

The Drivers: A Dialogue. Cambridge, printed for the author by Fletcher and Hodson and sold in London by J. Almon [and 4 others], 1770.

Dulany, Daniel, the Younger. *Considerations on the Propriety of Imposing Taxes in the British Colonies for the Purpose of Raising a Revenue by Act of Parliament.* North America, 1765; rpt. London: J. Almon, 1766.
Second edition, 1766.

Dummer, Jeremiah, the Younger. *A Defence of the New-England Charters.* London: Printed for J. Almon, [1765].

E--l of Ch----m's Apology. A Poem. London: Printed for J. Almon, 1766.

Election Flights. London: Sold by J. Almon [and others], [1780].
Second edition, 1780.

English Freeholder. *A Letter to the Earl of Bute upon his Union with the Earl of Chatham in Support of the Popular Measure of a Four-Shillings Land-Tax.* London: Printed for J. Almon, 1767.

Englishman. *Considerations upon the French and American War.* London: Printed for J. Almon, 1779.

————. *A Letter to Lord George Germain.* London: Printed for J. Almon, 1776.

————. *A Letter to the Whigs.* London: Printed for J. Almon, 1779.

————. *Pride: A Poem. Inscribed to John Wilkes.* . . . London: Printed for J. Almon, 1766.

An Enquiry into the Nature and Legality of Press Warrants. London: Printed for J. Almon, 1770.

An Enquiry into the Practice and Legality of Pressing by the King's Commission: Founded on a Consideration of the Methods in Use to Supply the Fleets and Armies of England. . . . London: Printed for J. Almon, 1772.

An Epistle to the Right Honourable Lord G--- G---. London: Printed for J. Almon, 1778.

An Essay on the Mortality of the Soul. London: Printed for J. Almon, 1775.

128

Estwick, Samuel. *A Letter to the Reverend Josiah Tucker. . . .* London: Printed for J. Almon, 1776.

Eumenes. *A Plan for the Government of Bengal and for the Protection of the Other British Settlements in the East Indies. . . .* London: Printed for J. Almon, 1772.

Evans, Caleb. *A Letter to the Rev. Mr. John Wesley, Occasioned by his Calm Address to the American Colonies. . . . A New Edition. To which are Prefixed Some Observations on the Rev. Mr. Wesley's Late Reply.* London: Printed for Edward and Charles Dilly and J. Almon, 1775.

Evans, Robert. *A Sermon Preached before the Right Hon. the Lord Mayor and the Worshipful the Court of Aldermen of the City of London. . . . On the 28th Day of September, 1771.* London: Printed for J. Almon, 1771.

The Examination of Doctor Benjamin Franklin, Relative to the Repeal of the American Stamp Act. 1766; rpt. London: Printed for J. Almon, 1767.

Extracts from the Votes and Proceedings of the American Continental Congress. Philadelphia, 1774; rpt. London: J. Almon, 1774.
Another edition, 1774.

A Fair Trial of the Important Question, or the Rights of Election Asserted . . . in which Two Pamphlets, Entitled The Case of the Late Middlesex Election, Considered, &c. And, Serious Considerations upon a Late Important Determination, are Very Fully Examined and Answered. . . . London: Printed for J. Almon, 1769.

Falconer, William. *An Address to Doctor Cadogan, Occasioned by his Dissertation on the Gout and Other Chronic Diseases. . . .* London: Printed for J. Almon, J. Wilkie, and F. Blythe, 1771.

The False Step; or the History of Mrs. Brudenel. A Novel. In Two Volumes. . . . London: Printed for J. Almon, 1771.

Father of Candor. *An Enquiry into the Doctrine, Lately Propagated Concerning Libels, Warrants, and the Seizure of Papers; with a View to Some Late Proceedings and the Defence of them by the Majority; upon the Principles of Law and the Constitution. In a Letter to Mr. Almon from the Father of Candor. [A Letter Concerning Libels, Warrants, the Seizure of Papers, and the Sureties for the Peace of Behaviour. . . .]* London: J. Almon, 1764.
Second edition, 1764.
Third, fourth, and fifth editions, 1765.
Another edition printed in Dublin, 1765.
Sixth edition, 1766.
Seventh edition, 1771.

La Fête Champêtre. London: Printed for J. Almon, 1774.
Second and third editions, 1774.

A Form of Sermon. . . . London: Printed for J. Almon, 1778.

Fragments and Anecdotes, Proper to be Read, at the Present Crisis. . . . London: Printed for J. Williams and J. Almon, 1764.

A Free Appeal to the People of Great Britain on the Conduct of the Present Administration since the Thirtieth of July, 1766. London: Printed for J. Almon, [1767].
Second edition, 1767.

Free, John. *The Analysis of Man. . . . A Sermon Preached at St. Mary's in Oxford before the University on Sunday, May 20, 1764. . . .* London: Printed for the author and sold by J. Almon [and others], [1764?].
Second edition, [1765?].

_____. *Matrimony Made Easy*. London: Printed for the author and sold by J. Almon [and others], [1764?].
Second edition, 1764.

_____. *The Operations of God and Nature. . . . A Sermon Preached before a Society of Florists. . . .* London: Printed for the author and sold by W. Sandby, J. Williams, and J. Almon, [1764].
Second edition, 1764.

Frequenter of Covent Garden Theatre. *The Conduct of the Four Managers of Covent-Garden Theatre . . . Examined, both with Regard to their Present Disputes and their Past Management.* London: Printed for J. Wilkie, J. Williams, and J. Almon, 1768.

The Fugitive Miscellany. Being a Collection of such Fugitive Pieces in Prose and Verse as are not in any Other Collection. With Many Pieces Never before Published. London: Printed for J. Almon, 1774–75.

Fugitive Pieces of Irish Politics, during the Administration of Lord Townshend. London: Printed for J. Almon, 1772.

Galloway, Joseph. *The Claim of the American Loyalists, Reviewed and Maintained upon Incontrovertable Principles of Law and Justice.* London: Printed by J. Almon, [1783?].

Gee, Joshua. *The Trade and Navigation of Great-Britain Considered. . . . A New Edition. . . .* 1729; rpt. London: Printed for J. Almon and S. Bladon, 1767.

The Genius of Britain. An Ode. In Allusion to the Present Times. London: Printed for J. Almon, 1775.

Gentleman at the Bar. *An Examination of the Rights of the Colonies, upon Principles of Law.* London: Printed for R. Dymott and J. Almon, 1766.

Gentleman, Francis. *The Sultan or Love and Fame. A New Tragedy.* London: Printed for J. Almon [and others], 1770.

Gentleman, Lately Retired from the Brewing Business. *Every Man his own Brewer. . . .* London: Printed for the author and sold by J. Almon and Mess. Robinson and Roberts, 1768.

Gentleman in Scotland. *Considerations on the Douglas Cause.* Edinburgh: Printed for J. Almon, London [and others], 1767.

Gentleman in a Select Society. *The Reply of a Gentleman in a Select Society upon the Important Contest between Great Britain and America.* London: Printed for J. Almon, 1775.

"George Washington." Engraving. Maryland, 1779; rpt. London: J. Almon [and others], 1780.

Georgicus. *The Letters of Georgicus upon the Iniquity of Tythes Intended for the Benefit of the English Farmer. . . .* London: Printed for J. Wilkie, J. Almon, and F. Blythe, 1773.

Graham, Catharine Macaulay. *Loose Remarks on Certain Positions to be Found in Mr. Hobbes' Philosophical Rudiments of Government and Society with a Short Sketch of a Democratical Form of Government in a Letter to Signior Paoli by Catharine Macaulay the Second Edition with Two Letters. . . .* London: Printed for J. Almon and [5 others], 1769.

Graham, James. *A Sketch: or, Short Description of Dr. Graham's Medical Apparatus. . . .* London: Printed and sold by Mr. Almon, Mr. Becket, and Messrs. Richardson and Urquhart, 1780.

Great Britain, Army, [Lists.] *The Military Register.* London: Printed for J. Almon [and others], [1772].

130

_____, Militia. [Lists.] *A List of the Officers of the Militia of England and Wales for the Year 1778.* London: Printed for J. Almon, 1778.

Great Britain, Board of Trade. *Report of the Lords Commissioners for Trade and Plantations on the Petition of the Honourable Thomas Walpole, Benjamin Franklin, John Sargent, and Samuel Wharton . . . for a Grant of Lands on the River Ohio . . . for the Purpose of Erecting a New Government.* London: Printed for J. Almon, 1772.

Great Britain, Court of Session. *The Speeches, Arguments, and Determinations of the Right Honourable the Lords of Council and Session in Scotland, upon that Important Cause, wherein His Grace the Duke of Hamilton and Others were Plaintiffs. . . .* London: Printed for J. Almon, 1767.

Great Britain, Parliament, House of Commons. [Lists.] *A Correct List of the Members of the Last House of Commons, Distinguished According to their Votes in Certain Late Public Questions in which the Rights and Liberties of the People were Essentially Concerned.* London: Printed for J. Almon and Debrett, 1780.

_____. [Proceedings.] *The Debate in the House of Commons on Wednesday, February 27, 1771 on the Bill to Repeal a Clause in the Act for Quieting the Possession of the Subject, Commonly Called the Nullum Tempus Act.* London: Printed for J. Almon, 1771.

_____. *The Debates and Proceedings of the British House of Commons.* (See Almon.)

_____. *Motions Made in the House of Commons on Monday, the 27th of March, 1775. Together with a Draught of a Letter of Requisition to the Colonies.* [London:] Printed for J. Almon, [1775].

_____. *The Parliamentary Register or History of the Proceedings and Debates of the House of Commons.* London: Printed for J. Almon and J. Debrett, 1781–96.

_____. *Report of the Lords of the Committee of Council. . . .* London: Printed by J. Almon, 1785.

_____. *Report from the Select Committee. . . .* London: Printed for J. Almon, 1778.

_____. *The Speech of a Right Honourable Gentleman, on the Motion for Expelling Mr. Wilkes, Friday, February 3, 1769.* London: Printed for J. Almon, 1769. Three more editions, 1769.

_____. *Substance of the Speeches. . . .* (See Burke.)

Great Britain, Parliament, House of Lords. [Proceedings.] *The Parliamentary Register or History of the Proceedings and Debates of the House of Lords.* London: Printed for J. Almon, 1775–80.

_____. *Protest against the Bill to Repeal the American Stamp Act, of Last Session.* Paris [i.e. London]: Chez J.W. [i.e. J. Almon], 1766.

Great Britain. [Treaties.] *A Collection of Treaties of Peace, Commerce, and Alliance between Great-Britain and Other Powers from the Year 1619 to 1734. To which is Added a Discourse . . . by the Right Hon. C. Jenkinson. . . . The Whole being a Supplement to A Collection of Treaties . . . from the Revolution in 1688. . . .* London: Printed for J. Almon and J. Debrett, 1781.

Greatrakes, William. *An Application of Some General Political Rules to the Present State of Great-Britain, Ireland and America. In a Letter to the Right Honourable Earl Temple.* London: Printed for J. Almon, 1766.

Greene, Edward Burnaby. *Cam. An Elegy.* London: Printed for J. Almon [and 5 others], 1764.

Greenwood, James. *A Rhapsody Occasioned by a Late Extraordinary Decision. . . .* London: Printed by J. Almon, J. Taylor, and J. Williams, [1775?].

Grenada Planter. *The Grenada Planter: or, a Full and Impartial Answer to a Letter in the Gazetteer of October 22, 1768. Relative to the Conduct of his Ex--cy G--r M--le.* London: Printed for J. Almon [and 3 others], [1768].

Grenville, George. *A Speech against the Suspending and Dispensing Prerogative, &c.* London: Printed for J. Almon, 1767.

Four more editions, 1767.

Grenville, Richard (Earl Temple). *The Principles of the Late Changes Impartially Examined: In a Letter from a Son of Candor to the Public Advertiser.* London: Printed for J. Almon, 1765.

Second edition, 1765.

Griffith, Elizabeth. *The Double Mistake. A Comedy.* London: Printed for J. Almon [and 3 others], 1766.

Second and third editions, 1766.

Griffith, Richard. *The Posthumous Works of a Late Celebrated Genius.* 2 vols. London: Printed by W. and J. Richardson and sold by J. Almon [and 3 others], 1770.

Hartley, David. *An Address to the Committee of Association of the County of York, on the State of Public Affairs.* York: Printed by A. Ward and sold by J. Almon, G. Kearsly, R. Faulder, London; R. Crutwell, Bath; and by all the booksellers in York, [1781]. Second edition, 1781.

———. *The Budget. Inscribed to the Man who Thinks himself Minister.* London: Printed for J. Almon, 1764.

Second through eighth editions, 1764.

Ninth and tenth editions, ?

Eleventh edition, 1766.

———. *Letters on the American War.* London: Printed for Almon [and others], 1778.

Second, third, and fourth editions, 1778.

Fifth edition, ?

Sixth, seventh, and eighth editions, 1779.

———. *The Right of Appeal to Juries in Causes of Excise, Asserted.* London: Printed for J. Almon, [1770?].

Second edition, [1770].

———. *Speech and Motions Made in the House of Commons on Monday, the 27th of March, 1775.* [London]: Printed for J. Almon, 1775.

Second edition, 1775.

———. *The State of the Nation, with a Preliminary Defence of the Budget.* [London]: Printed for J. Almon, 1765.

Four more editions, 1765.

———. *Substance of a Speech in Parliament. Upon the State of the Nation and the Present Civil War with America. Upon Monday, April 1, 1776.* London: Printed for J. Almon, 1776.

———. *Two Letters from D. Hartley . . . Addressed to the Committee of the County of York.* London: Printed for J. Almon, 1780.

An Heroic Congratulation Addressed to the Honourable Augustus Keppel. . . . London: Printed for the author and sold by J. Almon [and others], [1779].

Hervey, Augustus John (Earl of Bristol). *The Earl of Bristol's Speech, Taken Exactly Down as Spoken, in the House of Lords.* London: Printed for J. Almon, 1779.

Hippesley, R. *Bath and it's Environs, a Descriptive Poem, in Three Cantos.* Bath: Printed by R. Cruttwell, for J. Almon, London and W. Frederick, Bath, 1775.

Historical Memoirs of His Late Royal Highness William-Augustus, Duke of Cumberland. London: Printed for J. Almon [and 4 others], 1767.

Hodgson, Edward. *Short-hand Contractions.* . . . London: Printed for the author and sold by J. Almon [and 5 others], [1780?].

Holwell, John Zephaniah. *An East India Observer Extraordinary.* [London: Printed for John Almon?, 1767].

Hope, John. *Letters on Certain Proceedings in Parliament during the Sessions of the Years 1769 and 1770.* London: Printed by J. Almon, 1772.

Hopkins, Stephen. *The Grievances of the American Colonies Candidly Examined.* Providence, Rhode Island, 1765; rpt. London: J. Almon, [1766?].

Howe, William. *The Narrative of Lieut. Gen. Sir William Howe in a Committee of the House of Commons on the 29th of April, 1779, Relative to his Conduct during his Late Command of the King's Troops in North America.* . . . London: Printed by H. Baldwin. Sold by Almon and Debrett; P. Elmsley; and R. Baldwin, 1780.
Second edition, 1780.
Third edition, 1781.

Hulme, Nathaniel. *A Treatise on the Puerperal Fever: Wherein the Nature and Cause of that Disease, so Fatal to Lying-in Women, are Represented in a New Point of View Illustrated by Dissections; and a Rational Method of Cure Proposed.* . . . London: Printed for T. Cadell, G. Robinson, and J. Almon, 1772.

Hutchins, Thomas. *A Topographical Description of Virginia, Pennsylvania, Maryland, and North Carolina.* . . . London: Printed for the author and sold by J. Almon, 1778.

Hutchinson, Benjamin. *A Sermon Preached on Friday, February 27, 1778, the Day Appointed for a General Fast.* . . . London: Printed for J. Almon, 1778.

Ides, Simon. *The Eviad: A Burlesque Poem. In Two Cantos.* . . . London: Printed for J. Almon and J. Debrett [and 5 others], 1781.

The Importance of the British Dominion in India Compared with that in America. London: Printed for J. Almon, 1770.

Ireland, Parliament. House of Lords. [Proceedings. 1634–1770] *A Collection of the Protests of the Lords of Ireland, from 1634 to 1770.* London: Printed for J. Almon, 1771.

Jenings, Edmund. *Considerations on the Mode and Terms of a Treaty of Peace with America.* London: Printed for Edward and Charles Dilly and J. Almon, [1778?].
Second edition, 1778.

Jones, Henry. *Clifton: A Poem, in Two Cantos.* Bristol: Printed by E. Farley for the author and sold in London by Almon [and 4 others], 1767.

Jones, Rowland. *The Circles of Gomer, or an Essay towards an Investigation and Introduction of the English, as an Universal Language.* . . . London: Sold by J. Almon [and others], 1771.

———. *The Philosophy of Words.* . . . London: Printed by John Hughs and sold by Almon [and 7 others], 1769.

Jones, William. *The Constitutional Criterion.* . . . London: Printed for J. Almon, 1768.

Journal of the Proceedings of the Congress Held at Philadelphia, September 5th, 1774. London: Printed for J. Almon, 1775.

Journal of the Proceedings of Congress Held at Philadelphia from September 5, 1775 to April 30, 1776. Philadelphia; rpt. London: J. Almon, 1778.

The Justice and Necessity of Taxing the American Colonies, Demonstrated. London: Printed for J. Almon, 1766.

Kenrick, William. *Falstaff's Wedding: A Comedy.* The second edition. London: Printed for J. Almon [and 6 others], 1766.

Keppel, Augustus. *The Defence of Admiral Keppel.* London: Printed for J. Almon, 1779.

_____. *The Proceedings at Large of the Court-Martial, on the Trial of the Honourable Augustus Keppel, Admiral of the Blue. Held . . . January 7th, 1779. . . . Taken in Short Hand, by W. Blanchard, for the Admiral. . . .* London: Printed for J. Almon, 1779.

Ki'en Long. *A Chinese Imperial Eclogue. Translated from a Curious Oriental Manuscript. And Inscribed by the Translator to the Author of an Heroic Epistle to Sir William Chambers, Knight.* London: Printed for J. Almon, 1775.

Kimber, Edward. *An Extinct Peerage of England. . . .* London: Printed for J. Almon, 1769.

_____. *The Peerage of Ireland. . . .* London: Printed for J. Almon [and 8 others], 1768.

Knox, William. *An Appendix to The Present State of the Nation. Containing a Reply to the Observations on that Pamphlet.* London: Printed for J. Almon, 1769.

_____. *The Controversy between Great Britain and her Colonies Reviewed. . . .* London: Printed for J. Almon, 1769.

_____. *The Present State of the Nation: Particularly with Respect to its Trade, Finances, &c. &c. Addressed to the King and Both Houses of Parliament.* London: Printed for J. Almon, 1768.

Second and third editions, 1768.

Fourth edition, 1769.

L.T. *A Candid Enquiry into the Causes and Motives of the Late Riots in the Province of Munster in Ireland. . . .* London: W. Flexney, J. Almon, and F. Newbery, 1767.

Lambart, Richard. *A New System of Military Discipline Founded upon Principle.* London: Printed for J. Almon, 1773.

Langrishe, Hercules. *Considerations on the Dependencies of Great Britain. With Observations on a Pamphlet, Intitled The Present State of the Nation.* London: Printed for J. Almon, 1769.

Second edition, 1769.

"The Last Stake." Engraving. London: J. Almon, 1779.

The Late Occurrences in North America and Policy of Great Britain, Considered. London: Printed for J. Almon, 1766.

Lathrop, John, the Elder. *Innocent Blood Crying to God from the Streets of Boston. A Sermon. . . .* London: Printed for E. and C. Dilly and J. Almon, 1770.

Layman. *The Church an Engine of the State.* London: Printed for J. Almon and J. Bew, 1778.

Lee, Arthur. *An Appeal to the Justice and Interests of the People of Great Britain in the Present Disputes with America.* London: Printed for J. Almon, 1774.

Second and third editions, 1775.

_____. *Answers to Considerations on Certain Political Transactions of the Province of South Carolina.* London: Printed for J. Almon, 1774.

_____. *A Second Appeal to the Justice and Interests of the People, on the Measures Respecting America.* London: Printed for J. Almon, 1775.

_____. *A Speech, Intended to have been Delivered in the House of Commons, in Support of the Petition from the General Congress at Philadelphia.* London: Printed for J. Almon, 1775.

Lennox, Charles (3rd Duke of Richmond). *An Answer to A Short Essay on the Modes of Defence Best Adapted to the Situation and Circumstances of this Island.* London: Printed and sold by J. Almon, 1785.

134

A Letter from Albemarle Street to the Cocoa-Tree, on Some Late Transactions. London: Printed for J. Almon, 1764.
Second edition, 1764.
A Letter to the House of Commons; in which is Set Forth the Nature of Certain Abuses Relative to the Articles of Provisions. . . . London: Printed for J. Almon, 1765.
A Letter to Lord George Germaine, Giving an Account of the Origin of the Dispute between Great Britain and her Colonies. London: Printed for J. Almon, 1776.
Letter to a Minister on the Subject of the East India Dividend. London: Printed for J. Almon, 1767.
A Letter to the Right Honourable Lord North; on the East India Bill now Depending in Parliament. London: Printed for J. Almon; and Brotherton and Sewell, 1772.
A Letter to the Right Honourable Lord Pigot. London: Printed for J. Almon, 1777.
A Letter to the Right Honourable Viscount Cranborne. . . . London: Printed for J. Almon, 1780.
Letters from Portugal on the Late and Present State of that Kingdom. London: Printed for J. Almon, [1777].
Letters to and from the East-India Company's Servants. . . . London: Printed for J. Almon; P. Elmsly; and Brotherton and Sewell, 1772.
Liberalis. Two Letters. London: Printed for J. Almon, [1777].
Liberty Deposed, or the Western Election. A Satirical Poem. In Three Books. London: Printed for J. Almon, J. Williams, J. Coote and F. Blyth, [176?].
Liguier, Merchant of Marseilles. *What has been at all Times the Influence of Commerce upon the Genius and Manners of the People?* Translated from the French. London: Printed for J. Dodsley, J. Wilkie, and J. Almon, 1779.
The Lion Extricated. . . . London: Printed for J. Almon, 1777.
Lloyd, Charles. *The Conduct of the Late Administration Examined*. London: Printed for J. Almon, 1767.
Second edition, 1767.
———. *An Examination of the Principles and Boasted Disinterestedness of a Late Right Honourable Gentleman*. London: Printed for J. Almon, 1766.
———. *A True History of a Late Short Administration*. London: Printed for J. Almon, 1766.
Lloyd, Henry Humphry Evans. *An Essay on the Theory of Money*. London: Printed for J. Almon, 1771.
Lolme, Jean Louis de, of Geneva. *A Parallel between the English Constitution and the Former Government of Sweden*. . . . London: Sold by Almon, 1772.
Lonsdale, Mark. *The Spanish Rivals. A Musical Farce*. . . . London: Printed by J. Almon, 1784.
Lord Ch----m's Prophecy, an Ode Addressed to Lieutenant General G-ge. London: Printed for J. Almon, 1776.
Lord Knows Who. Verses Addressed to the ---- with a New Year's Gift of Irish Potatoes. London: Printed for J. Almon, 1775.
M. *Letters to Men of Reason and the Friends of the Poor on the Hardships of the Excise Laws Relating to Malt and Beer*. . . . London: Printed for J. Almon, 1774.
MacNally, Leonard. *Critic upon Critic: A Dramatic Medley*. . . . 2nd edn. London: Printed by J. Almon, 1792.
———. *Robin Hood; or, Sherwood Forest: A Comic Opera*. London: Printed by J. Almon, 1784.
A new edition, 1787.

Marat, Jean Paul. *Chains of Slavery*. London: Sold by J. Almon [and at least 2 others], 1774.

Second edition, 1774.

March, R. *A Treatise on Silk, Wool, Worsted, Cotton, and Thread*. London: Printed for the author and sold by J. Almon [and 3 others], 1779.

Marini, Giovanni Battista. *Cynthia and Daphne*. Translated from the Italian. London: Printed for the author and sold by J. Almon and W. Nicoll, 1766.

Marshall, Joseph. *Travels through Holland, Flanders, Germany, Denmark, Sweden, Lapland, Russia, the Ukraine, and Poland, in the Years 1768, 1769, and 1770*. London: Printed for J. Almon, 1772.

Martyn, Thomas. *A Letter to the Right Worshipful William Wynne*. . . . London: Printed for J. Almon and J. Bew, 1780.

Marvell, Andrew. *The Works of Andrew Marvell*. . . . London: Printed by Henry Baldwin and sold by Almon [and at least 11 others], 1776.

Mason, William. *An Epistle to Dr. Shebbeare: To which is Added an Ode to Sir Fletcher Norton*. . . . London: Printed for J. Almon, 1777.

Three more editions, 1777.

———. *An Heroic Epistle to Sir William Chambers*. . . . London: Printed for J. Almon, 1773.

Second through eleventh editions, 1773.

Twelfth edition, 1774.

Thirteenth edition, 1776.

Fourteenth edition, 1777.

———. *An Heroic Postscript to the Public, Occasioned by their Favourable Reception of a Late Heroic Epistle to Sir William Chambers*. . . . London: Printed for J. Almon, 1774.

Second through eighth editions, 1774.

Ninth edition, 1777?

Thirteenth edition, 1774.

———. *Ode to Mr. Pinchbeck, upon his Newly Invented Patent Candle-Snuffers*. . . . London: Printed for J. Almon, 1776.

Second through fifth editions, 1776.

Fifth(?) edition, 1777.

Massachusetts, General Court, House of Representatives. *The True Sentiments of America: Contained in a Collection of Letters Sent from the House of Representatives of the Province of Massachutts [sic] Bay to Several Persons of High Rank in this Kingdom*. . . . London: Printed for J. Almon, 1768.

Mellish, Mary. *The Trial of a Cause between Miss Mellish, Plaintiff; and Miss Rankin, Defendant. From Notes Carefully Taken in Court*. London: Printed and sold by J. Almon; sold also by J. Debrett and M. Massey, 1785.

Member of Parliament. *An Examination into the Conduct of the Present Administration from the Year 1774 to the Year 1778. And a Plan of Accommodation with America*. London: Printed for J. Almon, 1778.

Second edition, 1778.

———. *A Letter to the Right Honourable Lord M-----, on the Affairs of America*. London: Printed for J. Almon, 1775.

Meredith, William. *A Reply to the Defence of the Majority on the Question Relating to General Warrants*. London: Printed for J. Almon, 1764.

136

The Military Register; or New and Complete Lists of all his Majesty's Land Forces and Marines for the Year 1770. London: Printed for J. Almon [and 9 others], 1770.

Montcalm de Saint-Veran, Louis Joseph de, Marquis. *Letters from the Marquis de Montcalm, Governer-General of Canada. . . .with an English translation.* London: Printed for J. Almon, 1777.

Moore, John Henry. *The New Paradise of Dainty Devices: Consisting of Original Poems. By Different Hands.* London: Printed for J. Almon, 1777.

_____. *Poetical Trifles.* Bath: Printed by and for R. Cruttwell and sold in London by Almon, J. Dodsley, and Robson, 1778.

Another edition, 1778.

Second edition, Bath: Printed by and for R. Cruttwell and sold in London by F. Newbery, J. Dodsley, Robson, and Almon.

Morres, Hervey Redmond, Viscount Mountmorres. *Impartial Reflections upon the Question for Equalizing the Duties upon the Trade between Great Britain and Ireland.* London: Printed and sold by J. Almon, 1785.

Morris, Matthew Robinson-, Baron Rokeby. *Considerations on the Measures Carrying on with Respect to the British Colonies in North America.* The second edition with additions and an appendix. London: Printed for J. Almon [and 4 others], [1774].

Third edition, [1777?]

_____. *Peace the Best Policy or Reflection upon the Appearance of a Foreign War, the Present State of Affairs at Home and the Commission for Granting Pardons in America.* London: Printed for J. Almon, 1777.

The National Mirror. Being a Series of Essays on the Most Important Concerns but Particularly those of the East-India Company. London: Printed for Richardson and Urquhart; and John Almon, 1771.

The Necessity of Repealing the American Stamp-Act Demonstrated. London: Printed for J. Almon, MDCCLXVI [1765].

Neuhoff, Frederic de, Son of Theodore, King of Corsica. *Memoirs of Corsica.* London: Printed for S. Hooper and J. Almon, 1768.

A New Baronetage of England. 3 vols. London: Printed for J. Almon, 1769.

A New Edition of the Royal Kalendar. London: Printed for J. Almon [and 10 others], 1773.

The New Present State of Great Britain. London: Printed for J. Almon, 1770.

The second edition, 1776.

Noble Lord. *Liberty's Offering to British Electors.* London: Printed for J. Williams and J. Almon, 1768.

Nugent, Nicholas. *The Case of Nicholas Nugent, Esq., Late Lieutenant in the First Regiment of Foot Guards.* London: Printed for J. Almon, 1776.

Second edition, 1776.

O'Beirne, Thomas. *Candid and Impartial Narrative of the Transactions of the Fleet under the Command of Lord Howe.* London: Printed for J. Almon, 1779.

_____. *Considerations on the Late Disturbances, by a Consistent Whig.* London: Printed for J. Almon, 1780

Second and third editions, 1780.

_____. *Considerations on the Principles of Naval Discipline, and Naval Courts-Martial.* London: Printed for J. Almon and J. Debrett, 1781.

_____. *A Short History of the Last Session of Parliament, with Remarks.* London: Printed for J. Almon and J. Debrett, 1780.

O'Bryen, Denis. *The Prospect before Us.* London: Printed for J. Almon, 1788.
Third edition, 1788.
Observations on the Discourses Delivered at the Royal Academy. London: Printed for J.
Almon, 1774.
Observations on a Late Publication Entitled "Memoirs of Great-Britain, by Sir John Dalrymple."
London: Printed for J. Almon, 1773.
Observations on the Power of Climate over Policy, Strength, and Manners, of Nations. London:
Printed for J. Almon, 1774.
*Observations on Several Acts of Parliament, Passed in the Fourth, Sixth and Seventh Years of
his Present Majesty's Reign.* Published by the Merchants of Boston. Boston; rpt.
London: Reprinted for G. Kearsly, and J. Almon, 1770.
Another edition with variant title. *Observations of the Merchants at Boston in New-Eng-
land. . . .* [London: Printed for J. Almon], 1770.
An Ode to Peace Occasioned by the Present Crisis of the British Empire. London: Printed for
J. Almon, 1778.
*An Ode upon the Present Period of Time with a Letter Addressed to the Right Honourable George
Grenville.* London: Printed for J. Almon, 1769.
Officer. *A New System for the Establishment, Pay, Cloathing, Provisions, &c. &c. &c. of the
Army; Addressed to the Right Honourable Lord North. . . .* London: Printed for J. Almon,
1775.
Officer then Serving in the Fleet. *Candid and Impartial Narrative of the Transactions of the
Fleet under the Command of Lord Howe.* London: Printed for J. Almon, 1779.
The Optimist or Satire in Good-Humour. London: Printed for J. Almon, 1774.
*The Origin and Authentic Narrative of the Present Marratta War and also the Late Rohilla War,
in 1773 and 1774.* London: Printed for J. Almon and J. Debrett, 1781.
Osborne, Francis Godolphin (5th Duke of Leeds). *A Short Hint, Addressed to the Candid
and Dispassionate, on Both Sides of the Atlantic.* London: Printed for J. Almon, 1775.
Otis, James. *Considerations on Behalf of the Colonists.* London: Printed for J. Almon, 1765.
Second edition, 1765.
———. *The Rights of the British Colonies Asserted and Proved.* Boston; rpt. London:
Reprinted for J. Almon, [1764].
Second edition, [1765?].
———. *A Vindication of the British Colonies.* Boston, 1765; rpt. London: Reprinted for J.
Almon, 1769.
Paine, Thomas. *Common Sense.* Philadelphia, 1776; rpt. London: J. Almon, 1776.
Another edition, 1776.
Fourth edition, 1776.
Papers Laid before the House of Commons Relative to the Affairs of the East India Company. . . .
London: Printed for J. Almon, 1773.
Penn, James, Vicar of Clavering. *The Farmer's Daughter of Essex.* London: Printed for J.
Wilkie and sold by the author, J. Almon, F. Blyth; and W. Bingley, 1767.
———. *The Reasonableness of Repentance, with a Dedication to the Devil and an Address to the
Candidates for Hell.* London: Printed for the author and sold by J. Wilkie, J. Almon, F.
Blyth; and W. Bingley, 1768.
Philolethes. *The Pluralist, a Poem.* London: Sold by J. Almon [and at least 4 others],
1769.

Philonomos. [*Right Method of Maintaining Security.* . . .] *The Liberty of the Subject and Dignity of the Crown, Maintained and Secured without the Application of a Military, Unconstitutional Force.* . . . London: Printed for J. Almon [and 3 others], [1780?].

The Philosophy of the Passions. 2 vols. London: Printed for J. Almon, 1772.

Pilon, Frederick. *Barataria or Sancho Turn'd Governor, a Farce in Two Acts.* London: Printed by J. Almon, 1785.

_____. *The Fair American: A Comic Opera.* . . . London: Printed by J. Almon, 1785.

Pinto, Isaac de. *On Card-Playing. In a Letter from Monsieur de Pint[o] to Monsieur Didero[t].* London: Printed for J. Almon [and 3 others], 1768.

Pitt, William, Earl of Chatham. *Plan Offered by the Earl of Chatham to the House of Lords, Entitled A Provisional Act for Settling the Troubles in America and for Asserting the Supreme Legislative Authority and Superintending Power of Great Britain over the Colonies.* London: Printed for J. Almon, 1775.

Poems Fit for a Bishop. . . . *Inscription in Memory of the Earl of Chatham.* London: Printed for J. Almon, 1780.

Polignac, Melchior de, Cardinal. *A Translation of the Anti-Lucretius. By George Canning.* . . . London: Printed for the author and sold by J. Almon [and 9 others], 1766.

Political Speculations, or an Attempt to Discover the Causes of the Dearness of Provisions and High Price of Labour in England. . . . London: Printed for J. Almon, 1767.

Political Speculations. . . . *Part the Second.* London: Printed for J. Almon, 1767.

A Postscript to the Letter on Libels, Warrants, &c. in Answer to a Postscript in the Defence of the Majority and Another Pamphlet Entitled Considerations on the Legality of General Warrants. [London]: Printed for J. Almon, 1765.

The second edition, enlarged, 1765.

Another edition, 1765.

Pownall, Thomas. *A Letter from Governor to Adam Smith.* . . . London: Printed for J. Almon, 1776.

_____. *A Memoir Entituled Drainage and Navigation but One United Work.* . . . *Addressed to the Corporations of Lynn-Regis and Bedford Level.* London: Printed for J. Almon; and W. Whittingham, at Lynn, 1775.

_____. *A Memorial, Most Humbly Addressed to the Sovereigns of Europe on the Present State of Affairs between the Old and New World.* London: Printed for J. Almon, 1780.

Second edition, 1780.

_____. *The Right, Interest, and Duty of Government.* 1773; rpt. London: J. Almon, 1781.

_____. *A Topographical Description of such Parts of North America as are Contained in the (Annexed) Map of the Middle British Colonies, &c. in North America.* London: Printed for J. Almon, 1776.

_____. *Two Speeches of an Honourable Gentleman on the Late Negotiation and Convention with Spain.* London: Printed for J. Almon, 1771.

Second edition, 1771.

Pratt, Charles (Earl of Camden), supposed author. *Another Letter to Mr. Almon, in Matter of Libel.* London: Printed for J. Almon, 1770.

Second edition, 1771.

The Present State of the British Interest in India. London: Printed for J. Almon, 1773.

Private Letters from an American in England to his Friends in America. London: Printed for J. Almon, 1769.

The Privileges of the Island of Jamaica Vindicated; with an Impartial Narrative of the Late Dispute between the Governor and House of Representatives upon the Case of Mr. Olyphant, a Member of that House. Jamaica; rpt. London: Reprinted for J. Almon [and 3 others], 1766.

The Proceedings at Large of the Court-Martial on the Trial of the Honourable Augustus Keppel. London: Printed for J. Almon, 1779. (Issued simultaneously with *The Defence. . . .*)

A Prospect of the Consequences of the Present Conduct of Great-Britain towards America. London: Printed for J. Almon, 1776.

Protestant Gentleman. *A Dispassionate Enquiry into the Cause of the Late Riots in London.* London: Printed for J. Almon and J. Debrett, 1781.

Pye, Jael Henrietta. *A Peep into the Principal Seats and Gardens in and about Twickenham (the Residence of the Muses) with a Suitable Companion for those who Wish to Visit Windsor or Hampton-Court.* London: Printed for J. Bew; J. Almon; and G. Woodfall, 1775.

Pynsent's Ghost. London: Printed for J. Almon, 1766.

Ranelagh: A Poem. London: Printed for J. Almon, 1777.

Rayner, John. *A Digest of the Law Concerning Libels.* London: Sold by J. Almon [and 5 others], 1770.

"Read, Mark, Learn & Inwardly Digest." Engraving. London: J. Almon, 1780.

Reflections on the Case of Mr. Wilkes and on the Right of the People to Elect their own Representatives. To which is Added, the Case of Mr. Walpole. London: Printed for J. Almon, 1768.

Renwick, William. *The Genuine Distresses of Damon and Celia.* Printed in Bath for the author. London: Sold by Mr. Almon [and 4 others], 1771.

Rich, Robert, Bart. *A Letter from Sir Robert Rich . . . to the Right Honourable Lord Viscount Barrington, His Majesty's Secretary at War. To which is Added a Postscript. . . .* Second edition. London: Printed for J. Almon, 1776.

The Royal Kalendar or Complete and Correct Annual Register for . . . 1767. London: Printed for J. Almon [and 11 others], [1767].
Third edition, corrected, [1767].
Fourth edition, corrected, [1767].
Seventh edition, corrected, [1767].

The Royal Kalendar or Correct Annual Register for . . . 1768. London: Printed for J. Almon [and 12 others], [1768].

The Royal Kalendar or Complete and Correct Annual Register . . . for . . . 1769. London: Printed for J. Almon [and 11 others], [1769].

The Royal Kalendar or Complete and Correct Annual Register for . . . 1770. London: Printed for J. Almon [and 11 others], [1770].
Another edition, [1770].

The Royal Kalendar or Complete and Correct Annual Register for . . . 1771. London: Printed for J. Almon [and 11 others], [1771].

The Royal Kalendar or Complete and Correct Annual Register for . . . 1772. London: Printed for J. Almon [and 10 others], [1772].
Another edition, [1772].

The Royal Kalendar or Complete and Correct Annual Register for 1773. London: Printed for J. Almon [and 9 others], [1773].

The Royal Kalendar or Complete and Correct Annual Register for 1774. London: Printed for J. Almon [and 9 others], [1774].
Another edition, [1774].

The Royal Kalendar or Complete and Correct Annual Register for . . . 1775. London: Printed for J. Almon [and others], [1775]
Another edition, corrected, [1775].
The Royal Kalendar or Complete and Correct Annual Register for . . . 1776. London: Printed for J. Almon [and others], [1776].
Another edition, corrected, [1776].
The Royal Kalendar or Complete and Correct Annual Register for . . . 1777. London: Printed for J. Almon [and others], [1777].
Another edition, corrected. [1777].
Another edition, corrected, [1777].
The Royal Kalendar or Complete and Correct Annual Register for . . . 1778. London: Printed for J. Almon [and 12 others], [1778].
Another edition, corrected, [1778].
The Royal Kalendar or Complete and Correct Annual Register for . . . 1779. London: Printed for J. Almon [and 12 others], [1779].
Another edition, corrected, [1779].
The Royal Kalendar or Complete and Correct Annual Register for . . . 1780. London: Printed for J. Almon [and others], [1780].
Another edition, corrected, [1780].
Another edition, corrected, [1780].
The Royal Kalendar or Complete and Correct Annual Register for . . . 1781. London: Printed for J. Almon and J. Debrett [and 12 others], [1781].
Another edition, corrected, [1781].
Ruin Seize Thee, Ruthless King! A Pindaric Ode, Not Written by Mr. Gray. London: Printed for J. Almon, 1779.
Rustic [T.P. Andrews]. *A Letter to James Macpherson, Esq*. London: Printed for J. Almon, 1775.
Salignac de la Mothe Fenelon, Francois de. *The Adventures of Telemachus*. . . . Trans. Mark Meilan. 4 vols. London: Printed for the translator and sold by J. Almon, B. White, and J. Sewell, 1776.
Sappho. *A Poetic Rhapsody. Inscribed to the Fair Patroners of B-------h E-------n*. London: Printed for J. Almon, 1777.
A Satire. London: Printed for J. Almon, 1777.
Savile, Christopher. *The Case of Christopher Atkinson, Esq. . . .with a Complete Account of All his Commission Transactions with the Honorable Commissioners for Victualling His Majesty's Navy*. London: Sold by Almon; Robinson; Robson; Debrett; and Richardson, 1785.
————. *A Refutation of the Case of Christopher Atkinson, Esq*. London: Sold by J. Almon; J. Debrett; W. Flexney; and J. Sewell, 1785.
The Scotch Hut, a Poem Addressed to Euphorbus. . . . London: Printed for J. Almon, 1779.
A Select Collection of the Most Interesting Letters on the Government, Liberty, and Constitution of England which have Appeared in the Different News-papers from the Elevation of Lord Bute to the Death of the Earl of Egremont. London: Printed for J. Almon, 1763.
Second edition, 1763–64.
A Select Collection of the Most Interesting Letters on the Government, Liberty and Constitution of England which have Lately Appeared in the Public Papers. . . . Vol. 4. London: Printed for J. Almon, 1765.

A Series of Letters Addressed to the Greatest Politician in England: Containing a Description of Several Public Characters, a Defence of Sir George Saville and of Lord Chatham's Political Sentiments. . . . London: Sold by Mess. Almon and Debrett; and William Richardson, 1780.

A Sermon Preached in a Country Church on Friday, the 13th of December, 1776, the Day Appointed for a General Fast. London: Printed for J. Almon, 1776.

A Seventh Letter to the People of England: A Defence of the Prerogative Royal, as it was Exerted in His Majesty's Proclamation for the Prohibiting the Exportation of Corn. . . . [London]: Printed for the author and sold by J. Almon in Piccadilly and S. Bladon in Pater-noster-row, 1767.

Sharp, William, Jr. *An Englishman's Remonstrance: Inscribed to the Right Honourable Brass Crosby, Lord Mayor of London.* London: Printed for the author and sold by J. Almon, 1771.

Sharpe, William. *A Defence of Strictures on Dr. Lowth, Respecting Liberty.* The second edition, corrected. London: Printed for W. Flexney, G. Kearsly, and J. Almon, 1767.

———. *The Protestant or the Doctrine of Universal Liberty Asserted, in Opposition to Dr. Lowth's Representation of it.* . . . London: Printed for William Flexney, and J. Almon, [1766].

Sheridan, Charles Francis. *Observations on the Doctrine Laid Down by Sir William Blackstone Respecting the Extent of the Power of the British Parliament, Particularly with Relation to Ireland.* London: Printed for J. Almon; J Dodsley; and E. and C. Dilly, 1779. Second edition, 1779.

Sheridan, Richard Brinsley. *Verses to the Memory of Garrick.* London: Published by J. Almon [and 4 others], 1779.
Second edition, 1779.

Shore, Alured Henry. *A Letter to the Rev. Dr. Cooper on the Origin of Civil Government.* London: Printed for the author and sold by J. Almon and others, [1777].

A Short History of the Administration during the Summer Recess of Parliament. London: Printed for Fielding and Walker, and J. Almon, 1779.

A Short History of the Conduct of the Present Ministry with Regard to the American Stamp Act. London: Printed for J. Almon, 1766.

A Short History of English Transactions in the East-Indies. Printed for the author by Fletcher and Hodson in Cambridge; London: Sold by J. Almon; E. and C. Dilly, 1776.

A Short Narrative of the Horrid Massacre in Boston. . . . Printed by order of the town of Boston; rpt. London: Reprinted for E. and C. Dilly; and J. Almon, 1770.

Simes, Thomas. *A Military Course for the Government and Conduct of a Battalion.* . . . London: Printed for the author and Sold by Almon; Hooper; Richardson and Urquhart; and Walter, 1777.
Second edition, 1777.

———. *The Military Instructor.* . . . London: Printed for the author and sold by Millan; Almon; and Walker, Dublin, 1779.

———. *A Treatise on the Military Science.* . . . London: Printed by H. Reynell and sold by Almon [and 13 others in London], 1780.

Six Odes, Presented to that Justly-Celebrated Historian, Mrs. Catharine Macaulay. . . . Bath: Printed and sold by R. Cruttwell and sold also by E. and C. Dilly; J. Walter; T. Cadell; and J. Almon, London, [1777].

The Sixteenth Ode of the Third Book of Horace Imitated. With a Dedication to the Right Honourable the Lord N---h. [London]: Printed for J. Almon in Piccadilly; J. Bew in Paternoster-Row, and J. Sewell in Cornhill, 1777.

A Sketch of a Farce that may be Acted during the Parliamentary Recess by His Majesty's Servants. London: Printed for J. Almon, 1779.

Smart, Christopher, *Poems on Several Occasions.* London: Printed for the author and sold by Mr. Almon [and others], [1763].

Smith, William, Chief Justice of New York. *The History of the Province of New-York. . . .* London: Printed for J. Almon, 1776.

Smith, William, Provost of the College of Philadelphia. *An Oration in Memory of General Montgomery and of the Officers and Soldiers who Fell with him, December 31, 1775, before Quebec. . . .* Philadelphia; rpt. London: Reprinted for J. Almon, 1776.

Smollett, Tobias George, supposed author. *The History and Adventures of an Atom.* 2 vols. London: J. Almon, 1769.

Somers, John. *Jura Populi Anglicani or the Subject's Right of Petitioning Set Forth.* 1701; rpt. London: Reprinted for J. Almon, 1772.

_____. *The Security of Englishmen's Lives.* 1681; rpt. London: Printed for J. Almon, 1766. Another edition, 1771.

South Carolina. *Journal of the Provincial Congress. . . .* Charles-Town, 1776; rpt. London: J. Almon, 1776.

"Speedily will be Published." (See Rea, "Amelia Evans Barry.")

A Speech in Behalf of the Constitution against the Suspending and Dispensing Prerogative, &c. London: Printed for J. Almon, 1767.

Steele, Joshua. *An Account of a Late Conference on the Occurrences in America.* London: Printed for J. Almon, 1766.

Steel, Joshua. *An Essay towards Establishing the Melody and Measure of Speech to be Expressed and Perpetuated by Peculiar Symbols.* London: Printed by W. Bowyer and J. Nichols for J. Almon, 1775.

Stern, Philip. *Medical Advice to the Consumptive and Asthmatic People of England.* London: Printed for J. Almon, 1767.

Third edition, 1767.

Tenth and eleventh editions, 1771.

Fourteenth edition, 1774.

Sixteenth edition, 1776.

Twentieth edition, 1779.

Stevenson, John Hall. *An Essay upon the King's Friends, with an Account of Some Discoveries Made in Italy. . . . To Dr. S----l J-----n.* London: Printed for J. Almon, 1776.

_____. *Lyric Consolations. With the Speech of Alderman W---- Delivered in a Dream, at the King's Bench Prison the Evening of his Inauguration.* London: Printed for J. Almon, 1769.

_____. *Makarony Fables.* London: Printed for J. Almon, 1768.

Second and third editions, 1768.

Stock, William. *An Account of East-Florida.* London: Printed for J. Almon [and others], [1766].

Straightforward, Mrs. *A Letter from Mrs. Straightforward to her Son Timmy.* Printed for J. Deighton in Cambridge; London: Sold by Messrs. Rivington; and J. Almon, [1780?].

Straightforward, Timmy. *A Third Letter from Timmy Straightforward to his Mother. . . .* London: Sold by J. Almon; W. Cowper, Cambridge; and all other booksellers, [1780].

The System Occasioned by the Speech of Leonard Smelt. . . . London: Printed for J. Almon, 1780.

Second edition, 1780.

Thomas, William. *The Works of William Thomas, Clerk of the Privy Council in the Year 1549.* London: Printed for J. Almon, 1774.

Thompson, Edward. *The Soldier: A Poem Inscribed to the Honourable General Conway.* London: Printed for J. Almon, 1764.

Tooke, John Horne. *Facts: Addressed to the Landholders, Stockholders, Merchants, Farmers, Manufacturers, Tradesmen, Proprietors of Every Description, and Generally to all the Subjects of Great Britain and Ireland.* London: Printed for J. Johnson, and J. Almon, [1780].

Six more editions, 1780.

―――. *A Sermon.* London: Printed for J. Almon, 1769.

Second edition, 1769.

A Tour to Spa. . . . London: Sold by Almon [and 10 Others], 1774.

Townshend, Charles. *A Defence of the Minority in the House of Commons on the Question Relating to General Warrants.* London: Printed for J. Almon, 1764.

Four more editions, 1764.

The Triumph of Virtue and Beauty over Vice. London: Printed for the author and sold by J. Almon, 1775.

Trumbull, John. *McFingal: A Modern Epic Poem.* Philadelphia; rpt. London: Reprinted for J. Almon, 1776.

Trusler, John. *Chronology or a Concise View of the Annals of England.* London: Sold by J. Almon, 1769.

Tumulte de Londres, Commence le 2 Juin, 1780. Londres, imprime par H. Reynell et publie par J. Almon, Garrett, [1780].

Two Papers on the Subject of Taxing the British Colonies in America. London: Printed for J. Almon, 1767.

A View of the Several Changes Made in the Administration of Government since the Accession of His Present Majesty. London: Printed upon stamped paper, according to Act of Parliament, and sold by J. Almon, 1767.

Walpole, Horace, Earl of Orford. *A Counter-Address to the Public on the Late Dismission of a General Officer.* London: Printed for J. Almon, 1764.

Three more editions, 1764.

Walpole, Robert, Earl of Orford. *A Short History of that Parliament which Committed Sir Robert Walpole to the Tower, Expelled him the House of Commons, and Approved of the Infamous Peace of Utrecht.* London: Printed for J. Almon; and J. Williams, 1763.

Waring, John Scott. *An Epistle from Oberea, Queen of Otaheite, to Joseph Banks, Esq.* London: Printed for J. Almon, 1774.

Four more editions, 1774.

Watson, Richard, Bishop of Llandaff. *Chemical Essays.* Printed by J. Archdeacon in Cambridge; London: For J. Almon [among others], 1781–87.

―――. *A Discourse Delivered to the Clergy of the Archdeaconry of Ely on May 9th and 10th, 1780.* Printed by J. Archdeacon in Cambridge; London: Sold by J. Almon [among others], 1780.

Webb, Francis. *Thoughts on the Constitutional Power and Right of the Crown in the Bestowal of Places and Pensions.* London: Printed for G. Kearsly, and J. Almon, 1772.

West-India Planter. *Considerations on the State of the Sugar Islands. . . . In a Letter Addressed to the Right Hon. Lord North by a West-India Planter.* London: Printed for S. Bladon and sold by J. Almon; and Richardson and Urquhart, 1773.

Wharton, Charles Henry. *A Poetical Epistle to His Excellency George Washington. . . .* Annapolis, 1779; rpt. London: Reprinted for J. Almon [among others], 1780.

Wilkes, John. *The History of England from the Revolution to the Accession of the Brunswick Line.* London: Printed for J. Almon, 1768.

_____. *A Letter to His Grave the Duke of Grafton. . . .* London: Printed for J. Almon, 1767. Seven more editions, 1767.

_____. *A Letter to Samuel Johnson.* [London]: Printed for J. Almon, 1770.

Williams, David. *Lectures on the Universal Principles and Duties of Religion and Morality.* [London]: Printed for the author and sold by J. Almon [among others], 1779.

_____. *A Letter to the Body of Protestant Dissenters.* London: Printed for J. Almon; and J. Wilkie, 1777.

_____. *The Nature and Extent of Intellectual Liberty, in a Letter to Sir George Savile, Bart.* London: Printed for J. Almon [among others], 1779.

Williamson, Hugh. *The Plea of the Colonies on the Charges Brought against them by Lord M_____d and Others. . . .* London: Printed for J. Almon, 1775. Another edition, 1776.

Wilmot, John Eardley. *A Short Defence of the Opposition.* London: Printed for J. Almon; J. Dodsley; and B. White, 1778. Another edition, 1779.

Wright, Paul. *The Advantages of a Good Name and Godly End: A Sermon Occasioned by the Lamented Death of Isaac Whittington, Esq.* London: Sold by Mr. Almon [among others], [1773].

Yorke, Philip, First Earl of Hardwicke. *Two Speeches of a Late Lord Chancellor.* London: Printed for J. Almon, 1770.

Zenger, John Peter. *The Trial of John Peter Zenger, of New-York, Printer, who was Charged with having Printed and Published a Libel against the Government; and Acquitted. . . . To which is Now Added . . . the Trial of Mr. William Owen, Bookseller.* London: Printed for J. Almon, 1765.

Zubly, John Joachim. *The Law of Liberty: A Sermon on American Affairs Preached at the Opening of the Provincial Congress of Georgia. . . .* Philadelphia; rpt. London: Reprinted for J. Almon, 1775.

Index

Bette P. Goldstone

Lessons to be Learned

A Study of Eighteenth Century English Didactic Children's Literature

American University Studies: Series XIV, Education, Vol. 7.
ISBN 0-8204-0140-4   240 pp.   hardcover/lam. US $ 26.50
recommended prices – alterations reserved

Lessons to be Learned is a study of late eighteenth century English didactic children's literature. Through an investigation of social-historical trends, contemporary conceptualizations of childhood, reprinting data and critical reviews, the author shows that these books are far more important than previously believed. Stories by Mrs. Trimmer, Maria Edgeworth, Mrs. Barbauld, Mary Jane Kilner and Dorothy Kilner were not only read and enjoyed by many generations of children, but also helped define the genre of children's literature. *Lessons to be Learned* is invaluable for correcting misconceptions about this seminal literary period, and for raising important questions about how scholars should define and study children's literature.

Contents: A social-historical study of late eighteenth century English didactic children's literature – Critical literary reviews, discussions of social trends and biographies of authors are included.

PETER LANG PUBLISHING, INC.
62 West 45th Street
USA – New York, NY 10036